FLORENCE

Barbara Ender-Jones
and
Jack Altman

JPMGUIDES

Contents

This Way Florence

A Home for Genius

The grace and elegance of the Renaissance still linger on in the place that was once its workshop. Everywhere you go in this remarkable town, the stones call out the illustrious names of the past. When your ancestors have names like Dante, Medici and Michelangelo, you can hold your head a little higher.

In front of the old town hall, Palazzo Vecchio, the towering white nude statue of David has been decried by art-lovers as a monstrous replica of the magnificent original, which you can admire over in the Accademia's sculpture halls. But it does bear the stamp of the genius of Michelangelo. And in the galleries of the Uffizi, the paintings of Italy's greatest masters never fail to bewitch even the most blasé visitor, whether it be the acute perceptions of Giotto, the hypnotic mystery of Piero della Francesca or the seductive charm of Botticelli.

Time Out

But even in Florence, as they say, all art and no play… Don't overdo it, particularly in summer when the town's position in a basin of the Arno valley can make it a veritable simmering cauldron. Across from the Palaz-zo and the Uffizi, head for a soothing cup of cappuccino, a hot chocolate or one of those heavenly ice creams at the Café Rivoire. That, too, is Florence. Then wander among the goldsmiths on the venerable Ponte Vecchio, the oldest bridge across the sleepy waters of the Arno river. Along the banks of the river itself, sophisticated shops display finely tooled leather, handmade vellum stationery and grand antiques—exorbitant originals and impressive copies. Or you may prefer to check out the more modest leather goods and basketware of the bustling Mercato Nuovo.

Taking it easy in this town is very important if you want to avoid a bad case of cultural overdose—diagnosed by psychiatrists, quite seriously, as the Stendhal Syndrome, after the French novelist who fainted from too much artistic beauty in one morning. Take the Piazza del Duomo, for instance. Right there, even before you visit the cathedral, you have the Baptistery with not one but three pairs of monumental doors, with bronze panels fashioned by two of the greatest sculptors of their day—Lorenzo Ghiberti and Andrea Pisano. A few steps away is Giotto's beautiful soaring Campanile, also handsomely decorated with sculpted panels. The cathedral itself is crowned by one of the most beautiful domes in Christendom. And you haven't been inside yet. Feeling faint already?

In the Company of Great Men

The place which made Stendhal feel so queasy was the church of Santa Croce. Apart from the beauty of Brunelleschi's Pazzi Chapel, the Giotto frescoes and the Donatello sculptures, he had to contend with the tombs of Italy's immortals: Machiavelli, Michelangelo, Galileo and composer Rossini.

But one name more than any other has shaped the heart—and coolly reflective mind—of Florence: the Medici. You can feel the presence of this most powerful of Italian dynasties not only in the Uffizi, which began as the family business offices, but also in their family church, the San Lorenzo, in their palazzo and in their library, which was designed by Michelangelo. At their height, they almost made Florence a company town, the Medici company. In the streets around the church of San Lorenzo, Florentines today pay noisy homage to their greatest merchants with the town's most animated open-air market.

Room With a View

For a change of pace, the other, airier side of the river—Oltrarno to the Florentines—offers an opportunity to flee the crowds of the city centre. The aristocrats of old built their summer villas up on the heights among the pines and cypress trees. Today some of them are converted to luxury hotels. The Medici fortress, the Belvedere, seems to have been conceived, as the name suggests, more for its beautiful panorama of Florence and the surrounding Tuscan hills than for its defensive capacities.

Setting the style for the harmonious geometry of Florentine churches, the 12th-century San Miniato is a Romanesque jewel in green and white marble, but its terrace is also a magnificent vantage point for viewing the rest of the city.

The church of Santa Maria del Carmine needs no such pretext for a visit: art restorers have done an awesome job in retrieving the pristine beauty of the Masaccio frescoes in the Brancacci Chapel—you can't help but think that this is how Adam and Eve must have really looked.

Closer to the river, you can see another dimension of the Medici, where they swapped the discreet power of bankers for the plusher life of dukes in the Pitti Palace. The Pitti, divided into several museums,

Splashing through the Neptune Fountain in Piazza della Signoria.

houses the opulent family art collection. An hour or so there and you will be ready again for the relaxing antidote of the splendid Boboli Gardens, the dukes' back yard. Let the kids play around the fountains while you siesta under the trees.

Or plan a day trip out to Europe's loveliest suburb, Fiesole, amid gardens of cypress trees and olive groves. Beyond that, the whole of Tuscany beckons.

Hungry?

In a country not particularly reputed for its beef, Florence stands out for the steak-and-potatoes fraternity as champion of the gigantic T-bone *bistecca alla fiorentina*—charcoal-grilled in the middle of the trattoria. If you must have potatoes, they'll have to be a side-order, as this steak fills the whole plate. But the pasta here is great, too. Try the flat pappardelle noodles with a rich hare sauce. That's after the tasty little *crostini* of mashed chicken livers, or a hearty *ribollita,* bean and vegetable soup.

And of course you get the whole range of Tuscan wines to choose from—Chianti Classico or Montepulciano reds or the Vernaccia whites from San Gimignano.

Flashback

Roman Beginnings

The modern bustle of Piazza della Repubblica is a noisy echo of the forum and marketplace that were set up there by the Romans in 59 BC. The port of Florentia was established on the river Arno for goods carried between the Mediterranean and the old Etruscan strongholds around Arezzo. No monuments remain, though classical Roman urban design can still be seen in the grid-plan of streets crisscrossing in the city centre. You can also trace the outline of the Roman amphitheatre around the crescent of streets just west of Piazza Santa Croce.

Rise to Greatness

Florence did not become a force to be reckoned with until the 12th century. Its conquest of Fiesole and the systematic elimination of hostile fiefdoms in the surrounding hills forced the all-powerful German emperor, Frederick Barbarossa, to recognize its status and tax-gathering privileges as a commune. Florence grew rich on banking, trade and pioneering the manu-

San Miniato al Monte was built on the spot where an early Christian martyr set down his severed head.

facture of textiles on an industrial scale. It challenged Lucca's dominance of the silk trade and overhauled Siena's leadership in banking. The first Italian city to mint its own gold money, it naturally stamped its name, the florin, on the coin that was to become the gold standard for medieval and Renaissance Europe. The fierce rivalry with Siena was marked by two bloody battles: Siena's victory at Monteaperti in 1260 and Florence's brutal revenge at Colle di Val d'Elsa nine years later. Afterwards, other towns fell like dominoes.

To mark its new supremacy in Tuscany, Florence launched a huge building programme. This included the Palazzo Vecchio as an appropriately grandiose town hall, and the cathedral, with a campanile designed by Giotto. As part of the growing art boom, he was commissioned by the great banking families, the Bardi and Peruzzi, to paint frescoes for their private chapels in the church of Santa Croce.

Strife and Art

The patrician families hired mercenaries to fight in the vicious power struggles between the Guelph factions who sided with the pope and the Ghibellines supporting the German emperor. As a town councillor, Dante Alighieri got caught in the middle of a veritable civil war and had to flee the town in 1300. Florence lost a politician, and the world gained a poet—the man now acknowledged as the father of the modern Italian language wrote his *Divine Comedy* in exile.

Another literary work of art was the result of a second catastrophe. In 1348, the Black Death decimated the city's population, and the gentry took refuge in their country villas in the hills around Florence. They were joined by Giovanni Boccaccio, the son of a Florentine merchant family, who whiled away the time by composing the stories which became Italy's first masterpiece in prose form, *The Decameron*.

The Medici Reign

After the short-lived Ciompi uprising of wool-workers, the merchants reasserted control of city government. By the 1430s, the Medici banking family was pulling all the strings. If Lorenzo, the grandson, was to become the quintessential Renaissance prince, then Cosimo, founder of

DANTE

Durante Alighieri (1265–1321) was born to a bourgeois family of noble but poor descent; his father made a living by lending money. Dante fell in love with Beatrice Portinari when they were both nine years old. He remained devoted to her all his life, even though she did not return his love, married someone else and died in 1290. Dante describes this youthful passion in *La Vita Nuova*, a collection of lyric poems (1293). He studied the classics, religion and philosophy, and in 1295 married Gemma Donati, to whom he had been betrothed since the age of 12. The same year he joined the Guild of Physicians and Apothecaries, and soon became politically active during the struggles of the Guelphs and the Ghibellines. In 1301, as prior of Florence and the leader of a group of Guelphs, he was sent on an embassy to the pope in Rome and never returned home. He was banished from Florence in 1309 and sentenced to death in his absence. He finally settled in Ravenna. During his exile he wrote the epic poem *Divina Commedia* (*Divine Comedy*), a spiritual testament narrating a journey through Hell and Purgatory and finally to Paradise, guided by Beatrice. Writing in Italian rather than in Latin, Dante became a champion of the use of the Italian language as a vehicle for great art. Shortly after finishing the *Divine Comedy*, he died of malaria and was buried at Ravenna. He had seven sons and one daughter, Antonia, who became a nun, taking the name of Sister Beatrice.

the dynasty, was a Renaissance Godfather—but perhaps closer to an American big-city political boss than a Mafia *capo di capi*. Very much the iron fist in a velvet glove, he wielded his power behind the scenes in the Palazzo Medici. Without actually killing them, he made his opponents offers they could not refuse: knuckle under or get out of town. Then he destroyed their palazzi, leaving them no stronghold to return to. Meanwhile, Brunelleschi was giving the cathedral its dome, Ghiberti designing the Baptistery doors and Masaccio painting the Brancacci Chapel frescoes.

Lorenzo the Magnificent (1469–92) ruled Florence during the golden age of its Renaissance. Leonardo da Vinci, Botticelli, Michelangelo and architect Giuliano da Sangallo all worked under the Medici patronage, as did philosophers such as Pico della Mirandola. Magnificent, perhaps, but Lorenzo was no Mr Nice Guy. When an assassination attempt on him failed, he had 300 suspected accomplices executed, hanging a ringleader and the Archbishop of Pisa naked from a window of the Palazzo Vecchio.

Bonfire of the Vanities

In 1494, fanatical Dominican preacher Girolamo Savonarola led a moral backlash against the

LORENZO DE MEDICI

Lorenzo il Magnifico—the Magnificent—was short-sighted, had no sense of smell and spoke through his nose. The statesman and ruler, born in Florence (1449–92) was a great patron of literature and art. A brilliant diplomat but hopeless administrator, he wrote exalted poems, collected precious stones and antique statues, was a protector of artists and scientists, founded the Laurentian Academy, and was responsible for several calamitous bankruptcies.

irreligious licence which had accompanied the Florentine Renaissance. Taking advantage of a French invasion of Italy which drove the Medici rulers out of the city, Savonarola headed a theocratical dictatorship declaring Jesus to be King of Florence. With classic totalitarian methods, his police punished people for singing bawdy songs rather than Christian hymns, got children to denounce their parents and servants to spy on masters, drove Jewish money-lenders from the city and replaced them with Catholic pawnbrokers.

The high point of Savonarola's reign was the bonfire he organized in 1497 in front of the Palazzo Vecchio, onto which guilt-ridden aristocrats threw robes, jewels and cosmetics,

VASARI

Architect, painter and writer, Giorgio Vasari (1511–74) was a man of many talents, though it was said he excelled in none. In the service of the Medici family, he designed the Uffizi and the famous Corridor, painted the frescoes in Cosimo I's throne room and part of the cupola in the Duomo. But he achieved fame by writing a major reference work, *The Lives of the Most Eminent Italian Architects, Painters and Sculptors* (1550). And it was Vasari who invented the term "Renaissance".

musicians their instruments, Botticelli his paintings and Andrea della Robbia his sculpture. But the hostile pope's threat to Florentine property on church lands prompted the business-minded city fathers to hang Savonarola a year later. His bonfire was rekindled to burn the body.

Medici Comeback

The Medici had always been careful to keep in with the Vatican. Family power in Florence was restored thanks to Lorenzo's foresight in having his son Giovanni made a cardinal with the support of Pope Julius II. In 1513, Giovanni became Pope Leo X and had Michelangelo build the Medici family chapel in the church of San Lorenzo.

Cousin Giulio, archbishop of Florence, became Pope Clement VII ten years later, blessing the city with the works of Michelangelo and the rascally sculptor Benvenuto Cellini.

Caught up in international power struggles with the German empire, the Medici had to bow out in 1527. When the Habsburg emperors brought them back in the 1530s it was only as the puppet dukes of Tuscany. Lacking the discreet but real power of his namesake and founding father, Grand Duke Cosimo I had to settle for pomp and circumstance. The family moved their home across the river to the Pitti Palace, building an extension of the Palazzo Vecchio as their business offices, the Uffizi. Life was more showy now, and the court artists, painters Pontormo and Bronzino, sculptors Cellini and Giambologna, were more brilliant than masterful. The breath of genius had expired, and the Medici dukes could do little more than give terrific parties in the Boboli Gardens.

The dynasty sputtered to an end in 1737 with heirless Grand Duke Gian Gastone, an alcoholic gambler surrounded at court by 400 *ruspanti* (toy-boys). His widowed sister Anna Maria Luisa, last of the Medici family, bequeathed their collections to the city of Florence.

Behind its unassuming façade, San Lorenzo church is full of treasures, such as this little cupola.

Under Foreign Rule

In the 18th century, the Habsburgs moved the government of Tuscany from Florence to Vienna. The town became a cultural and political backwater, and building ground to a halt. A couple of archdukes dropped by, but the Florentines did not warm to their alien ideas of "enlightened despotism" surveyed by a garrison of soldiers from Lorraine and Lombardy.

In 1799, Napoleon Bonaparte's revolutionary army was welcomed as a breath of fresh air. Though the people liked the new ideas of national identity, they did not know what to make of the Frenchman's decision to make Florence capital of the "Kingdom of Etruria", and later of the decidedly less highsounding *département* of the Arno.

The Austrians returned in 1814. As part of their programme to modernize Tuscany, a railway was built in the 1840s by Scottish engineer Robert Stephenson, son of George, linking Florence to Pistoia, Pisa and Livorno. Florence also boasted Italy's first telegraph line, to Pisa. But these innovations did not seduce a population contaminated by the nationalist ideas of the French. A popular uprising forced Archduke Leopold II to flee in 1848. He came back with an army the next year, but unrest grew again and he was driven out for good in 1859, abandoned by his troops.

Independence

Artists and writers meeting in Florentine coffee houses had made the town a cultural capital of the Risorgimento independence movement. With Rome tied down by the conservative papacy, the new Italian king, Vittorio Emanuele resided briefly at the Pitti Palace, and the Palazzo Vecchio housed the newly independent nation's first parliamentary assemblies in 1861.

In keeping with the new urbanism of the 19th century, Florence replaced its old city walls with boulevards. On the south bank of the Arno, the great Piazzale Michelangelo was built to provide a grand view of the old city. But in the historic centre itself, space for what is now the clumsy Piazza della Repubblica was created by razing the beloved old market and scores of medieval houses. And the cathedral and church of Santa Croce were at last completed.

Modern Times

Florence has had a troublesome 20th century, but its spirit has always repaired the damage. In the Fascist era of Mussolini's dictatorship, the town was subject to conflicts between rightwing factions, largely Catholic, and left-wing partisans, mostly Communists, culminating in the bloody street battles of 1943. As World War II approached its climax, the retreating German army tried to slow the Allied advance by blowing up the city's bridges across the Arno, except the Ponte Vecchio. Even there, they destroyed old houses at each end. After the war the bridges were all rebuilt, and in the case of the Ponte Santa Trinita with much of the original 16th-century masonry hoisted back up from the river bed.

In 1966, the town suffered terrible flooding when the Arno overflowed its banks and destroyed or damaged hundreds of paintings, sculptures and priceless manuscripts. Flower Children of the hippie years—the Angels of Mud—waded in to help salvage Florence's artistic heritage. Then in 1993, the Mafia hit out blindly with a bomb smashing into the Uffizi Gallery. It ruined several masterpieces, but the building was repaired and reopened to the public within weeks, and restorers have applied all the miracles of modern technology to resurrect the damaged paintings and sculpture. Florence deals in the stuff of immortality.

Sightseeing

N o other city in the world can boast such a concentration of works of art. There are so many marvels in Florence that you would need several months to see them all. We have divided the city into five areas, to help you plan your sightseeing.

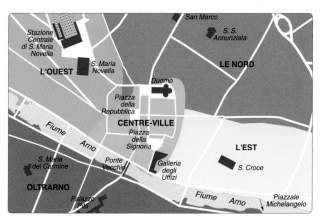

CITY CENTRE

Starting at the cathedral, we follow the essential sights in a clockwise direction, ending at the Piazza della Repubblica in the middle of the shopping district.

Duomo E 3*

: Piazza del Duomo
: Mon–Fri 10 a.m.–5 p.m.;
: Thurs 10 a.m.–4 p.m.;
: Sat 10 a.m.–4.45 p.m.;
: 1st Sat of month to 3.30 p.m.;
: holidays 1.30–4.45 p.m.

The Piazza del Duomo lies at the crossroads of the busiest streets in Florence. The great cathedral, built in the form of a Latin cross, takes up most of the space, its bright marble—white from Carrara, green from Prato, pink from Maremma— startling in contrast to the sombre ochres and greys of surrounding buildings.

Work on the cathedral—named Santa Maria del Fiore for the lily, symbol of Florence—was begun by Arnolfo di Cambio (1296) and continued after his death by Giotto, Francesco Talenti and others. The huge dome, built in 1436, was designed by Filippo Brunelleschi, and with its vast proportions— 48 m (157 ft) in diameter and 55 m (180 ft) high—is an architectural masterpiece.

The three airy, virtually unadorned aisles emphasize the echoing immensity of the interior, surprisingly bare and cold. When Savonarola used to preach here, he drew a congregation of 10,000 people!

On the inner façade, look for the clock painted with four heads of the Prophets by Paolo Uccello in 1443, and to the left of the entrance, a painting by Domenico di Michelino, *Evocation of Dante.* Below the high altar is a bronze shrine by Lorenzo Ghiberti containing relics of Saint Zanobius, one of the first bishops of Florence. Ghiberti also designed the round windows. The fresco inside the dome, depicting the *Last Judgment*, was painted by Vasari and Zuccari, and finished in 1579.

For a stunning panorama of the city, climb up to the lantern by the 463-step staircase running partly between the outer and inner shells of the dome. Seats are provided at the top. Undergoing restoration.

Campanile di Giotto D 3

: Piazza del Duomo
: Daily 8.30 a.m.–6.50 p.m.

To check museum opening times, call Firenze Musei 055 294 883.

Standing apart from the Duomo, the elegant bell-tower was designed by Giotto, who began its construction in 1334. He died three years later, and his pupil Andrea Pisano took over. The last three floors were finished by Francesco Talenti. You can clearly distinguish the change of style at each stage, as each architect added his personal touch.

The tower is 85 m (280 ft) high. Climb the 416 steps winding up to the top, to enjoy a superb panorama over the cathedral dome, the city and its surroundings.

Battistero D 3

Piazza San Giovanni
Daily 12.15–6.30 p.m.;
holidays 8.30 a.m.–1.30 p.m.

Dating from the 4th and 5th centuries, the octagonal Baptistery is without doubt the most ancient building in Florence: it influenced Renaissance architecture in Tuscany. The green and white marble facing was added during the 11th to 13th centuries.

It's fascinating to sit on the cathedral steps and watch people carefully inspecting the three magnificent doors of gilded bronze, which trace the evolution of Florentine sculpture from Gothic to Renaissance. The south doors (1328–38) are the work of Andrea Pisano, a pupil of Giotto. Lorenzo Ghiberti began work on the north doors in 1403; the panels recount the life of Christ. The result so pleased the Florentines that he was commissioned for the east doors in 1425. It took him more than 25 years to complete the doors, whose ten large square panels illustrate scenes from the Old Testament, including the creation of Adam and Eve, Noah's ark and Moses receiving the Ten Commandments. They greatly impressed Michelangelo, too, who declared them "Doors of Paradise", a name that has stuck. Imagine the scene in 1966 when the flood waters of the Arno were strong enough to unhinge the doors and sweep some of the panels more than 2 km away! In fact those you see here are copies; the originals are kept in the Museo dell'Opera del Duomo.

Inside the Baptistery, the walls are clad in marble, and the cupola is covered in scintillating mosaics by several artists, including Cimabue, Coppo and Giotto. An octagon indicates the spot where children used to be baptised on New Year's Eve. To the right of the altar, the tomb of Antipope John XXIII is by Donatello and Michelozzo.

Outside the Baptistery, the stone
Column of Saint Zanobius

marks the place where a withered elm tree once stood. When, in 1429, the saint's remains were transferred from the basilica of San Lorenzo to a church outside the city walls, the coffin brushed against the elm which subsequently burst into leaf.

San Salvatore al Vescovo D 3

- Piazza dell'Olio
- Tel. 055 271 071
- Open two weeks per month, 4–7 p.m. Phone for details.

Typical of Florentine polychrome architecture, the marble façade of this little Romanesque church was inspired by the decoration of the Baptistery. It dates from the 12th century. The fresco in the choir is the work of Giovanni Domenico Ferretti (18th century).

Museo del Bigallo D 3

- Piazza San Giovanni 1
- Tel. 055 215 440
- Daily (except Tues) 10 a.m.– 1.30 p.m. and 3–6.30 p.m.

This small palace dating from 1352–58 houses a collection of 14th–16th-century religious works of art, and paintings by Tuscan artists. Sculpture by Alberto Arnoldi is displayed in the magnificent Gothic loggia, which in medieval times was used to show lost or abandoned children for adoption.

Museo dell'Opera del Duomo E 3

- Piazza del Duomo 9
- Tel. 055 230 2885
- Mon–Sat 9 a.m.– 6.50 p.m.;
- Sun 9 a.m.–1 p.m.

If the Duomo and Baptistery seem cavernous and empty, that's because all their treasures were transferred to this museum, opened in 1891. Here you can see choir lofts sculpted by Luca della Robbia and Donatello, works by Ghiberti, Pollaiuolo and Michelangelo (including the *Pietà* he intended for his tomb). Also on display are the tools used by Brunelleschi to build the dome, his wooden models of the dome and lantern—and his death mask. In the courtyard, now covered over with glass, Michelangelo sculpted his statue of *David*.

Casa di Dante Alighieri E 4

- Via Santa Margherita 1
- Tel. 055 219 416
- Tues–Sat 10 a.m.–5 p.m., Sun 10 a.m.–1 p.m. Closed last Sun of month

Dante Alighieri, author of the epic poem *Divine Comedy*, haunts the streets just south of the cathedral. This house reconstructed between

The heart of the city, Santa Maria del Fiore.

1875 and 1910 is said to be his birthplace, though there's nothing to prove it and the original building has disappeared. A small museum recounts his life and work.

Badia Fiorentina E 4
Via del Proconsolo

This ancient Benedictine abbey was founded in 978 and extended by Arnolfo di Cambio from 1285. Among the many features of the interior, admire the Gothic ceiling, the tombs, and a splendid canvas by Filippino Lippi, *The Virgin Appearing to Saint Bernard*. Don't miss the adjoining Orange-Tree Cloister (Chiostro degli Aranci), bathed in medieval serenity.

Museo Nazionale del Bargello E 4
Via del Proconsolo 4
Tel. 055 238 8606
Daily 8.15 a.m.–1.50 p.m.
Closed 1st, 3rd, 5th Sundays, 2nd and 4th Mondays of each month

This imposing medieval fortress, dating from the 13th–14th centuries, was the city's first town hall. It became the seat of the magistrates responsible for law and order, whose coats of arms adorn the courtyard. In the 16th century it housed the offices of the chief of police, or Bargello. The building also served as a prison in the 18th century. It now contains a splendid sculpture collection, with works by Michelangelo, Cellini, Sansovino and Giambologna as well as Donatello's bronze *David*, the first nude statue of the Renaissance, and Verrocchio's *David*, with the head of Goliath between his feet. You can also see the original bronze panels designed by Ghiberti

---

TOWER HOUSES

Wealthy Florentines of the 12th century lived in *case-torri*, great square towers reaching in some cases to a height of 70 m (230 ft). A law was introduced in 1250 to limit the height to 25 m (82 ft). With their narrow doors and small windows they were easy to defend; a network of wooden walkways linked one house to another so that the inhabitants could visit their neighbours when the streets were impassable. The holes in the façades where the scaffolding was lodged are still visible. A large group of *case-torri* is to be seen in Via del Corso, at the corner of Via Santa Elisabetta (D 3). Others are in the nearby streets: the Pagliazza in Via Santa Elisabetta, the Casa Lapi at the corner of Via de' Cerchi, the Casa de' Cerchi at the corner of Via del Canto alla Quarconia. You will come across others south of the river, if you take a walk along Borgo San Jacopo (C 5)

and Brunelleschi when they were competing for the commission of the Baptistery doors. There are also several small collections, as charming as they are varied: Renaissance jewellery, Venetian glass, ivories, majolica and small bronzes.

Piazza della Signoria D 4

In Florence all roads lead to the Piazza della Signoria, the political and administrative centre of town. It is dominated by the Palazzo Vecchio, seat of the city council, and the Torre di Arnolfo, 94 m (308 ft) high, added in 1310. On the south side of the square is the Loggia della Signoria (or dei Lanzi), built in the late 14th century and now sheltering several statues, including two works by Giambologna and a magnificent bronze *Perseus* by Cellini. The roof of the loggia is the terrace of the Uffizi's café. In front of the Palazzo Vecchio stands a copy of Michelangelo's *David* and a 16th-century marble group of *Hercules and Cacus* by Baccio Bandinelli. The statue of Neptune surmounting the fountain (Fontana del Nettuno) is the work of Bartolomeo Ammannati, between 1560 and 1575. The Florentines have always found the gigantic white figure of the sea god

to be a little too pallid, and gave him the irreverant nickname Biancone. The water-nymphs at his feet are by Giambologna, who also sculpted the nearby equestrian statue of Cosimo I.

Palazzo Vecchio D 4

Piazza della Signoria
Tel. 055 276 82 24
Daily 9 a.m.–7 p.m.; Thurs and holidays 9 a.m.–2 p.m.; in summer Mon and Fri late closing 11 p.m.

Built between 1298 and 1314 to plans drawn by Arnolfo di Cambio, the fortress-like Old Palace (or Palazzo della Signoria) is the very symbol of the city. Initially the seat of the supreme magistrature (the Signoria) in 1293, it changed its function several times. It was renamed the Palazzo Vecchio when the Medici family moved over the river to the Palazzo Pitti. The courtyard was decorated with frescoes of Austrian cities after the marriage of Cosimo I's son to an Austrian princess. An impressive staircase by Vasari leads to the Salone dei Cinquecento (1495) where meetings of the city council were held, and where the first parliament of a united Italy met. The walls and ceiling are covered in frescoes by Vasari, and there's an exceptional statue of *Victory* by Michelangelo.

Do not miss the delightful Studiolo di Francesco I, designed by Vasari and covered with painted panels representing Earth, Water, Fire and Air. The same elements are depicted in the Quartiere degli Elementi on the second floor.

You can also see the apartments of Eleonora, Cosimo I's wife, but the highlight is the 15th-century Sala dei Gigli (Hall of the Lilies), decorated with heraldry, gilt-panelled ceiling and frescoes by Ghirlandaio.

The original of Donatello's bronze *Judith and Holofernes* also stands here; the one in the piazza outside is a copy.

Uffizi D 5

Piazzale degli Uffizi 6
Tel. 055 294 883
Daily (except Monday)
8.15 a.m.–6.35 p.m.

This vast U-shaped building, with the short side overlooking the Arno, was begun in 1560 by Vasari on the orders of Cosimo I to house the business offices of the Medici family. However, as soon as they moved in, they set aside rooms on the top floor for their personal collection of paintings. It was bequeathed to the city of Florence in 1737 by Anna Maria Ludovica, the last member of the illustrious dynasty.

MICHELANGELO

The fourth son of Ludovico and Francesca Buonarroti Simoni, a wealthy Florentine couple, Michelangelo was born in Caprese on March 6, 1475. He was sent to a wet-nurse in Settignano, a small village above Florence in hills pocked by quarries. He spent all his boyhood in this family of stone-masons; instead of going to school he learned how to use the hammer and chisel. Returning to his parents at the age of 10, he began to study but showed a clear preference for drawing. Finally he persuaded his father to apprentice him to Domenico Ghirlandaio, Florence's most fashionable painter at the time.

Michelangelo placed sculpture at the top of the artistic hierarchy, and had unlimited admiration for those who were able to release the figures hidden within the blocks of marble. He never married, claiming that art was his mistress. "My children", he said, "are the works I leave behind me, for even if their value is modest, they will survive a while." On his deathbed (in 1564), he lamented that he was dying at the precise moment when he was beginning to understand the rudiments of his profession.

This extremely popular gallery contains more than 1700 works displayed in 45 rooms. Hung in chronological order, they trace the evolution of European art since the 13th century, to which was added recently the Contini Bonacossi Donation comprising prestigious paintings and sculpture.

The setting alone, with frescoed and panelled ceilings and walls, even in the corridors, is so stunning you really have to concentrate to take in the details of the paintings. Make sure you have plenty of time in hand. Note that rooms are occasionally closed for restoration; these are indicated on a board near the ticket office. At the end of the circuit is a pleasant café, with an outdoor terrace overlooking the Piazza della Signoria.

The first rooms display a succession of religious paintings. Look, in particular, for:
Cimabue (1280) and Giotto (1310): retables depicting the Virgin Mary;
Gentile da Fabriano: *Adoration of the Magi* (1423); Masaccio: *Saint*

Anne Metterza (1424); Fra Angelico: *Crowning of the Madonna* (c.1430) Paolo Uccello: *Battle of San Romano* (c.1456); Filippo Lippi: *Madonna and Child* (c. 1465).

Then come more diversified works: Piero della Francesca: *Portrait of the Duke of Urbino* (c.1465) Antonio Pollaiuolo: *Hercules and the Hydra* (c. 1475); Botticelli: *Spring* (1478), *Birth of Venus* (1485), *Madonna of the Magnificat* (1481); Leonardo da Vinci: *Annunciation* (1472); Michelangelo: *Holy Family with San Giovannino* (1504); Raphael: *Madonna of the Goldfinch* (1506); Andrea del Sarto: *Madonna of the Harpies* (1517); Dürer: portrait of the artist's father;

Michelangelo: Holy Family with St Giovannino (1504).

Cranach: portrait of Luther, *Adam and Eve;*
Titian: *Madonna of Urbino;*
El Greco: *Two Saints;*
Rubens: portrait of his wife;
Caravaggio: *Bacchus;*
Rembrandt: two self-portraits.

Corridoio Vasariano D 5

⋮ Visits by appointment;
⋮ tel. 055 238 8651

This "corridor" snakes over an entire kilometre, from the second floor of the Palazzo Vecchio, through the Uffizi, alongside the river and over the boutiques of the Ponte Vecchio, to the Palazzo Pitti. Commissioned by Cosimo I, who lived in constant fear of assassination, it was built in a record five months by Giorgio Vasari. The corridor made a perfect safety route between the old and new palaces. From the beginning its walls were hung with paintings. The 17th- and 18th-century works include a magnificent series of self-portraits, and among the artists represented are Boucher, Gentileschi, Lorenzo Lippi and Rosalba Carriera, who specialized in pastels.

The austere Italian Gothic exterior of the Palazzo Vecchio is by Arnolfo di Cambio.

Santo Stefano al Ponte D 5

⋮ Piazza Santo Stefano

In a tiny medieval square, this church dates from the 11th century. The door and the windows are typically Florentine Romanesque in style, and framed with green and ivory marble.

Ponte Vecchio D 5

Spanning the Arno at its narrowest point, Florence's oldest and most picturesque bridge has been destroyed several times by floods but it was spared in 1944 when all the other bridges were blown up by the Germans. Today's construction dates from 1345. Originally the shops were occupied by fishmongers, butchers and tanners, who swept all their waste into the river. In 1594 Duke Ferdinand did away with this smelly commerce and replaced the traders with jewellers and goldsmiths, many of whom increased their space by building extensions over the parapet. One of the symbols of Florence, the bridge has open arcades in the middle so you can enjoy a view of the river.

Ponte Santa Trinita C 4–5

This elegant bridge adorned with statues representing the Four Seasons was built in 1257, and it's said that the legendary first meeting between Dante Alighieri and Beatrice took place here. It was demolished by the Germans in 1944, but the original stones were retrieved from the Arno and used to rebuilt it in 1954.

Santa Trinita C 4

- Piazza Santa Trinita
- Mon–Sat 9 a.m.–noon and
- 3.30–6 p.m.

This church was built in the 11th century and enlarged in the 13th, and Buontalenti added a baroque façade in the late 16th century. Among the church's treasures, the tomb of Bishop Benozzo Federighi is one of Luca della Robbia's finest achievements. But the most striking works of art are the Ghirlandaio frescoes in the Sassetti Chapel, to the right of the choir, illustrating *Scenes of the Life of St François*. Sassetti, whose porphyry tomb is adorned with ox heads, was a banker, at the head of the Medici companies.

Museo dell'Antica Casa Fiorentina C 4

- Palazzo Davanzati
- Via Porta Rossa 13
- Closed for restoration

The Davanzati Palace, converted into a museum, illustrates the daily life of a wealthy Florentine family in the 14th century. Furniture and utensils date from the 14th to 19th centuries. Unusually for the time, the house is supplied with sanitation and water on every floor, drawn from a well by an ingenious system of buckets and pulleys. The Sala dei Pappagalli—a dining room decorated with frescoes—is particularly beautiful.

Mercato Nuovo D 4

- Logge Mercato Nuovo
- Daily (except Sunday and
- holidays) 8 a.m.–7 p.m.

Beneath a Renaissance loggia, built in the mid-16th century to shelter goldsmiths and silk merchants, the New Market is famous for its Florentine straw articles—hats, baskets, chairs and decorative objects. But you'll also see racks of leather jackets, bags and shoes, ceramics and various knicknacks. Look for the famous **Fontana del Porcellino** (1612): the "little pig" is in fact a wild boar. Rub his nose and throw a coin in the fountain and you will soon come back to Florence.

Orsanmichele D 4

- Via Arte della Lana 1
- Daily (except Mon) 10 a.m.–5 p.m.

Built between 1337 and 1350, this church was originally a shop and grain market. Hollow pillars allowed grain to be poured from the upper floors down to the loggia. The ground floor arcades were walled in and decorated in Florentine Gothic style when the loggia was transformed into a church in 1367. The interior is dominated by a superb marble tabernacle by Andrea Orcagna, surrounding a painting of the Virgin and Child attributed to Bernardo Daddi, a pupil of Giotto. The outside niches hold statues of the patron saints of various guilds. The church is open to visitors, despite the ongoing restoration.

Piazza della Repubblica D 3–4
A large chunk of medieval Florence, the ghetto and old marketplace were razed at the end of the 19th century to make space for this airy, arcaded piazza. The Colonna della Dovizia marks the crossroads of the old Roman thoroughfares, the *cardo* and *decumanus*. Through the archway on the west side is Via degli Strozzi. The square is a favourite meeting place for the Florentines. A flower market, **Mercato delle Piante**, is held on Thursdays under the loggia of the central post office.

FASHION

The centre for high fashion has moved to Milan, but there are two shows per year at Florence's Palazzo Pitti, which attract world-wide attention.

The great designers all have boutiques in or around **Via dei Tornabuoni** (C 3–4). Ferragamo's headquarters are in the handsome Spini Feroni palace, at no 14. The palace also houses the Salvatore Ferragamo Museum, relating the history of this prestigious fashion house. Visits Mon–Fri 9 a.m.–1 p.m. and 2–6 p.m. The jeweller Pomellato is at no. 89, Gucci at 73–75, and Crisci Tanino, who makes fine boots and shoes by hand, at 43–45.

Round the corner in **Via della Vigna Nuova**, you will notice Emilio Pucci's shop at no. 97—the silks are designed by the Marquis and produced in his workshop on traditional looms. Halfway along the same street, on Piazza dei Rucellai, you'll find Zegna Ermenegildo, proposing everything for the smart man about town.

Via degli Strozzi boasts the fourteen shop windows of Principe, an institution for Florentine fashions (nos. 21–29). The splendid palace of the **Arte della Lana**, near Orsanmichele church, houses the high-quality designs of Zanobetti, in the business for three generations.

Other streets focussing on fashion are Via dei Calzaiuoli, Via dei Cerretani, Via Roma and Via Calimala, all around the Duomo, and, just across the Arno, along Via Guicciardini and Borgo San Jacopo.

WEST OF CENTRE

This is largely a commercial area, dominated by the main railway station, nearby bus station and chaotic traffic. Amid the big buildings, however, are some gems worth seeking out.

Galleria Corsini C 4
Palazzo Corsini
Via del Parione 11
Tel. 055 212 880
Open by appointment

One side of the palace gives onto the Lungarno (quay) Corsini. It contains a splendid private collection with works by Pontormo, Raphaël, Rigaud and other Italian and European artists of the 15th–18th centuries.

Ognissanti B 3
Piazza Ognissanti
Cloister and refectory
open Mon, Tues, Sat
9 a.m.–noon

This church was built at the end of the 13th century by the Guild of Wool Weavers: wool was the basis of Florentine prosperity. The façade of 1637 was one of the first works in baroque style in the city. The richly decorated interior includes a fresco by Domenico Ghirlandaio and a painting from the school of

Giotto. In one of the rooms of the 15th-century cloister (entrance at no. 42) is a famous fresco of *The Last Supper* by Ghirlandaio.

Santa Maria Novella C 2
Piazza Santa Maria Novella
Mon–Thurs, Sat 9 a.m.–5 p.m.
Fri and Sun 1–5 p.m
Chiostri Monumentali daily
(except Friday) 9 a.m.–5 p.m.

Dominican architects began building here in 1279, on the site of an ancient church. The façade (undergoing restoration) is entirely covered in inlaid marble, and shows a combination of Romanesque, Gothic and Renaissance influences. Inside, the three aisles were rebuilt by Vasari in 1565. There are several important works such as a wooden crucifix by Giotto, Masaccio's *Holy Trinity* of 1427 (left aisle), frescoes by Ghirlandaio in the Tornabuoni Chapel *(Apparition of the Angel to Zachariah in the Temple)*, a marble pulpit by Brunelleschi and many other chapels filled with treasures. At the church exit, a baroque gateway at no. 18b leads to the **Chiostri Monumentali**. These remains of the ancient monastery are a haven of peace, welcome respite from the noise and bustle of the area. The Chiostro Verde (Green Cloister) is so called because of the dominant colour of Paolo Uccello's frescoes, *The Flood* and *the Story of Noah*. The Cappellone degli Spagnoli (Chapel of the Spaniards), by Talenti, was the chapterhouse of the monastery. It has frescoes (1367) by Andrea da Firenze. At no. 16 of nearby Via della Scala, the **Officina Farmaceutica di Santa Maria Novella** is an 18th-century pharmacy selling all kinds of fragrant lotions and potions.

MNAF C 3
- Museo Nazionale Alinari della Fotografia Leopoldine
- Piazza Santa Maria Novella 14a
- Tel. 055 216 310
- Daily (except Wed) 9.30 a.m.– 7.30 p.m., Sat to 11.30 p.m.

Founded on the collections of the Alinari brothers, one of Florence's most famous photography firms, this new museum housed in a prestigious 16th-century building documents the evolution of photography since its origins in 1839, through its Golden Age to the Avant-Garde and modern times. The MNAF includes an innovative Touch Museum with 20 photographs reworked in Braille; sign-language interpreters available for groups of 10–15 people.

Cascine (off map by A 2)
- Bus no. 17c

Catch a bus and ride out to this shady park stretching along the river bank just beyond Piazza Vittorio Veneto. The Medici owned farms *(cascine)* here, and the land was turned into a public park in the 18th century. Florentine families love to come here to relax on public holidays, especially at Ascension for the Festa del Grillo (Grasshopper Festival).

There are several fountains and several unusual constructions dotted around, such as a pyramid and, at the park's western tip, a monument to the Maharaja of Kolhapur. The racetrack was built in 1966.

On Tuesday mornings, a lively outdoor **market** is held in the Cascine, selling fresh produce, household articles and clothing.

Fortezza da Basso
- Viale Filippo Strozzi
- (off map by C 1)
- Open only for special exhibitions

The biggest historical monument in Florence was commissioned by Alessandro de' Medici, the first Duke of Florence. The five-sided fortress (built 1533–35) was the work of Antonio da Sangallo the Younger. It no longer protects the city from foreign invaders: the terrace is used for craft and commercial exhibitions.

NORTH OF CENTRE

Between San Lorenzo and San Marco spreads the University district, full of interesting specialist shops and friendly neighbourhood bars and cafés.

Santa Maria Maggiore D 3
Via de' Cerretani

The interior of this 12th-century church contains some Gothic features restored at the beginning of the 20th century, with baroque decoration of the 17th–18th centuries. The most beautiful work of art in the church is a 13th-century polyptych of the *Virgin and Child* in the left-hand chapel; it is attributed to Coppo di Marcovaldo.

San Lorenzo D 2
Piazza San Lorenzo
Mon–Sat 10 a.m.–5 p.m.
Sun (March–Oct) 1.30–5 p.m.

Begun in 1419, this Renaissance church is the collective effort of the great artists of the city's Golden Age. It contains numerous masterpieces including a marble tabernacle of 1460 and two bronze pulpits by Donatello.

Reached through the left transept, the **Old Sacristy** is the work of Brunelleschi and Donatello, who was responsible for the sculpted

elements. Look up at the dome of the small chapel, painted with the signs of the zodiac.

The **New Sacristy** (access from Piazza Madonna degli Aldobrandini) was Michelangelo's first architectural work: of particular note are the sculptures on the sarcophagi and the statues of Lorenzo and Giuliano Medici. The Medici family ceremonies were celebrated in this church: their tombs are contained in the **Medici Chapels** (access from Piazza Madonna degli Aldobrandini, closed alternately Sunday or Monday). The **Cappella dei Principi** (Chapel of the Princes), sumptuously clad in rare marbles and mosaics of precious stones, is not to be missed.

Biblioteca Laurenziana D 2
Piazza San Lorenzo 9
Tel. 055 210 760
Daily (except Mon) 9.30 a.m.–1.30 p.m.

To the left of the entrance to the church of San Lorenzo, this celebrated library was designed by Michelangelo to house the collections of manuscripts acquired by Cosimo the Elder and his sons Piero and Lorenzo. The monumental staircase, begun by Michelangelo, was completed by Vasari and Ammannati.

Mercato di San Lorenzo D 2

- Via dell'Ariento and Piazza San Lorenzo
- Daily 9 a.m.–7 p.m.
- Closed Sun and Mon in winter

Clustering around the church and spreading around the nearby streets, this is the biggest and most popular of Florence's markets. It's a good place to find a bargain pair of shoes.

Mercato Centrale D 1

- Piazza del Mercato Centrale
- Daily (except Sun) 7 a.m.–2 p.m.; Sat to 5 p.m.

The monumental building (1870–74) was designed by a Milanese architect, Giuseppe Mengoni, and combines brick and glass in a framework of cast iron. The market is devoted entirely to food.

Palazzo Medici-Riccardi D 2

- Via Cavour 3
- Daily (except Wednesday)
- 9 a.m.–7 p.m.

Michelozzo was commissioned to build this palace for Cosimo de' Medici between 1444 and 1464, and it became the model for all the great Florentine palaces of the Renaissance. In 1659 the Medici sold it to the Riccardi who enlarged the building and renovated the interior in baroque style. In 1814 the palace was sold to the State. Since then it was used for administrative offices, and the Provincial Governor still occupies premises here.

The highlight of the palace is the lovely Medici Chapel of the Magi, decorated with a cycle of frescoes by Benozzo Gozzoli in the 15th century. The Chamber of Lorenzo the Magnificent has been converted into an interactive multimedia consultation room with state-of-the-art PointAt system technology developed by the University of Florence. The digitalized Gozzoli frescoes are projected onto a large screen; you just have to point at any part of the painting you want to see in greater detail.

The late-17th century Riccardi Gallery is in baroque style, with frescoes by Luca Giordano celebrating the Medici family. The ground floor rooms of the palace house a Medici museum, where you can see the will of Anna Maria Ludovica, the last of the line, stipulating that the Medici treasures should never leave Florence.

Museo dell'Opificio delle Pietre Dure E 1

- Via degli Alfani 78
- Tel. 055 265 111
- Mon–Sat 8.15 a.m.–1.50 p.m.

The workshop was created in 1588 by Cosimo de' Medici, who brought the best craftsmen in Europe to Florence to create inlaid mosaics of marble and semi-precious stones. Many ancient works of art are restored here today. The small museum displays exquisite examples of the craft, from table tops to curiosity cabinets. Upstairs you can follow all the stages in creating a mosaic, beginning with the initial drawings, progressing to selecting the coloured stones, cutting, fitting them together like a jigsaw puzzle, and the final polishing.

Galleria dell'Accademia di Belle Arti E 1

Via Ricasoli 60
Tel. 055 238 8609
Daily (except Monday) 8.15 a.m.–6.20 p.m.

The world-famous statue of *David*, sculpted by Michelangelo in 1501 when he was 25, found a home here in the Academy of Fine Arts in 1873 after having weathered almost four centuries in front of the Palazzo della Signoria. The rooms house sculpture and paintings from the 13th to the 18th centuries, with more sculptures by Michelangelo (notably the unfinished *Four Slaves*, who look as though they are struggling to escape from their mantle of rough marble), and works by Domenico di Michelino, Ghirlandaio and Botticelli, among many more.

San Marco E 1

Piazza San Marco 1
Tel. 055 238 8608
Daily 7–11.30 a.m., 3.30–6 p.m.
Museo di San Marco daily 8.15 a.m.–1.50 p.m.; 2nd and 4th Sun of each month 8.30 a.m.–7 p.m. Closed 2nd and 4th Mon of each month.

Comprising church, convent and cloisters, this complex dating from 1299 is grouped behind a baroque façade overlooking a busy square. The convent is now one of the city's most interesting museums, with many paintings and frescoes by Fra Angelico, was a monk here.
In the Pilgrim's Hospice, to the right of the entrance, you can see some fine retables and altar paintings, and an enchanting wooden panel originally intended as a cupboard door, with 35 small paintings including an *Annunciation* where the Angel Gabriel has wings striped in red, blue and yellow. Beyond the

Lorenzo the Magnificent depicted as one of the Three Kings in a fresco by Gozzoli (Palazzo Medici-Ricardi).

frescoed cloister, the Small Refectory is decorated with a mural by Ghirlandaio of *The Last Supper*. In the upstairs dormitory, each of the monks' tiny cells is adorned with a different fresco by Fra Angelico or his pupils. At the head of the stairs is the luminous *Angel of the Annunciation*. In some of the cells, parts of the floor have been removed and mirrors artfully placed so you can see traces of ancient paintings underneath.

At the end of the cells to the right of the stairs you can visit Cosimo de' Medici's "duplex", where he came to meditate, while round at the other end are Girolamo Savonarola's quarters, with his desk and black hooded cloak. The library, also upstairs, was designed by Michelozzo and displays illuminated books.

Chiostro dello Scalzo
- Via Cavour 69 (off map by E 1)
- Mon, Thurs, Sat 8.15 a.m.– 1.50 p.m.

This small 16th-century cloister, sometimes just called Lo Scalzo, is famous for its monochrome frescoes by Andrea del Sarto. They were commissioned by the Brotherhood of St John the Baptist, also called Scalzo (bare-footed) as the members went bare-foot in processions.

Il genio di Leonardo E 2
- Via dei Servi 66/68r
- Tel. 055 282 966
- Daily 10.30 a.m.–6.30 p.m. in winter, 10 a.m.–7 p.m. in summer

Functioning, life-size models of Leonard's machines faithfully reproduced from his drawings.

Giardino dei Semplici Orto Botanico F 1
- Via Micheli 3
- Daily (except Wed) 9 a.m.– 1 p.m.; Sat 9 a.m.–5 p.m.

The Herb Garden, founded in 1545 by Cosimo I, is one of Europe's foremost botanical gardens. The Medici grew exotic plants here and studied the extraction of essential oils. It still grows rare plants.

Santissima Annunziata F 1
- Piazza della Santissima Annunziata
- Daily (except Wed) 9 a.m.–noon, 4–5 p.m.

Built around 1250 by the founders of the Servite Order (the Order of the Servants of Mary), this church was rebuilt and renovated in the 17th and 18th centuries. It was once a centre of pilgrimage famed throughout Europe. Do not miss the frescoes by Rosso Fiorentino, Andrea del Sarto *(The Nativity of Mary)* and Pontormo, nor the magnificent carved wooden ceiling and a small marble temple made to a design by Michelozzo.

Museo dello Spedale degli Innocenti F 1

- Piazza della Santissima Annunziata 12
- Tel. 055 203 7308
- Daily 8.30 a.m.–7 p.m.,
- Sun to 2 p.m.

The building, by Brunelleschi, was an orphanage. Today it contains important frescoes and other works of art, among them the *Adoration of the Magi* by Ghirlandaio and the *Virgin and Child* by Botticelli.

Museo Archeologico F 1

- Via della Colonna 38 (entrance Piazza SS Annunziata 9)
- Tel. 055 235 75
- Mon 2–7 p.m.;
- Tues, Thurs 8.30 a.m.–7 p.m.
- Wed, Fri–Sun 8.30 a.m.–2 p.m.

On three floors of the 17th-century Palazzo della Crocetta, this museum houses Etruscan, Greek, Roman and Egyptian collections. You can also see the newly opened Maria Maddalena de Pazzi corridor linking the palace to the Santissima Annunziata church.

Cimitero degli Inglesi H 1

- Piazzale Donatello

The gate will probably locked but you can ring for admittance to this leafy cemetery, the last resting place of the poetess Elizabeth Barrett Browning and many other British expats.

Santa Maria Maddalena dei Pazzi G 2

- Borgo Pinti 58
- Daily 8.30 a.m.–7 p.m.,
- holidays 8.30 a.m.–2 p.m.

Originally constructed by Giuliano da Sangallo, this church was entirely rebuilt in 1628. The interior is decorated with frescoes. Perugino's *Crucifixion* covers a whole wall of the chapter house.

Museo Topografico "Firenze Com'era" E 3

- Via dell'Oriuolo 24
- Tel. 055 276 8224
- Mon–Wed 9 a.m.–2 p.m.,
- Sat 9 a.m.–7 p.m.

To see how the city has evolved, walk down to the museum of "Florence as it was", south of the Santa Maria Novella hospital. It is housed in an old monastery. The exhibits trace the city's architectural history from the 15th to the 19th centuries by means of engravings, paintings, postcards and photographs. The fourteen semi-circular paintings, or "lunettes", by Justus Utens (1599), depicting the Medici villas and gardens, are of particular interest.

EAST OF CENTRE

The area around Santa Croce still has a medieval feel to it, especially in the narrow streets around Borgo dei Greci and Via Torta. You'll discover antique dealers and carpenters' workshops, and near the Teatro Verdi, on the site of the former prison (Stinche), Florence's most famous *gelateria*. The Medicis used to stage jousts on the huge Piazza Santa Croce, lined on one side with a row of buildings with cantilevered and frescoed upper storey.

Casa Buonarroti F 4

- Via Ghibellina 70
- Tel. 055 241 752
- Daily (except Tuesday)
- 9.30 a.m.–2 p.m.

Michelangelo drew the plans for this small palace, which he had built on a plot of land bought in 1508. You will see drawings by the master himself, his letters and portraits, works of his youth and a collection of 17th-century paintings illustrating his life.

Mercato delle Pulci G 4

- Piazza dei Ciompi
- Daily 10 a.m.–1 p.m.,
- 3.30–7.30 p.m.

You may not find the bargain of the year in this flea market, but it's always fun to browse through the old postcards and prints, and to rummage through the stalls.

Mercato di Sant'Ambrogio G 4

- Piazza Ghiberti
- Daily (except Sunday)
- 7 a.m.–2 p.m.

This market held in a 19th-century cast iron building sells fresh produce, flowers, clothing, shoes, and second-hand goods.

Santa Croce F 5

- Piazza Santa Croce
- Mon–Sat 9.30 a.m.–5.30 p.m.;
- Sun and public holidays
- 1–5.30 p.m.

STONE AND MARBLE

The Florentine hills are studded with quarries, and there have always been ample supplies of hard stone for its religious and civil buildings. Local grey and ochre stone could be cut easily into shape and was most often used for construction and decoration. The harmony of their colours was enhanced by polychrome cladding of green serpentine, gravel and marble. White marble—pure, recrystallized limestone—from Carrara is appreciated all over the world for its lustre and smooth texture which makes it ideal for statuary. Coloured veins are caused by the presence of other minerals.

The largest Franciscan church in the city was designed by Arnolfo in 1294; it took 100 years to build. The immense Gothic nave contains the tombs of many celebrated Italians, including Michelangelo (inside the door to the right), designed by Vasari and with seated allegorical figures of Painting, Sculpture and Architecture. Galileo, Machiavelli and Ghiberti are also entombed here. The nineteen chapels harbour numerous treasures and have beautiful stained-glass windows. To the right of the altar, the Bardi and Peruzzi chapels are decorated with frescoes by Giotto, the first illustrating the life of St Francis, and the second that of St John.

Museo dell'Opera di Santa Croce F 5

- Piazza Santa Croce 16
- Tel. 055 24 46 19
- Mon–Sat 9.30 a.m.–5.30 p.m.,
- Sun and public holidays 1–5 p.m.

The church museum, in the cloisters, houses works by the great Florentine masters such as Donatello, Bronzino and others. The famous *Crucifix* by Cimabue, seriously damaged in the floods of 1966 is here, meticulously restored, and you can also admire Andrea Orcagna's frescoes of the *Last Judgment*. Outside the museum stands a memorial to the Lady with the Lamp, Florence Nightingale.

Museo della Fondazione Horne E 5

- Palazzo Corsi-Alberti
- Via dei Benci 6
- Tel. 055 244 661
- Daily (except Sunday and holidays) 9 a.m.–1 p.m.

In 1916, an English architect generously bequeathed this small 15th-century palace to the city of Florence, together with its entire exquisite collection of furniture, ceramics and Renaissance works of art.

FLORENTINE CERAMICS

This industry flourished in the 15th century, first with the production of objects used for medical purposes, then with more varied articles for a private clientele. But in the second half of the century, small towns around Florence, such as Monte-lupo, began to offer a wider choice in models and colours. Wealthy families and nobles ordered bowls, jugs, plates and bowls painted with their coats of arms; their preferred colours were blue, green and orange. The Cafaggiolo school, founded at the beginning of the 16th century, was famous for the extreme elegance of its shapes and its decorative motifs.

OLTRARNO

When you have explored the Pitti Palace and rested a while in the Boboli Gardens, walk along the river bank and up to Piazzale Michelangelo, for a painterly view of the city. From here you can catch the bus no. 13 which will sweep you through the hills and back to the city centre.

Santa Felicita C 6
- Piazza Santa Felicita

A church was built on this spot in the 4th century, on the site of an ancient cemetery. It was rebuilt several times and finally renovated in 1736 in a classical style. It became the Medici's church when the family moved to the Palazzo Pitti, and they reached it via Vasari's Corridor, which enabled Cosimo to partake in mass from a lofty balcony without having to mingle with the congregation.
The Capponi Chapel, the first on the right, was designed by Brunelleschi and decorated by Jacopo Pontormo, whose *Deposition* (1528), in intense pinks and blues, is especially famed.

Palazzo Pitti C 6
- Piazza Pitti
- Via Guicciardini

- Information and booking: tel. 055 294 883

This is the largest of the Florentine palaces, its façade stretching 205 m (224 yd) along the square. Begun in 1457 by Brunelleschi on the orders of Luca Pitti, a banker and rival of the Medici, the palace was inherited by Eleonora di Toledo, wife of Cosimo I de' Medici. King Vittorio Emanuele II of the House of Savoy lived here in 1860 when Florence was capital of Italy. Today the palace comprises numerous museums and galleries.

Appartamenti Reali
- Tel. 055 238 8611
- Daily (except Monday)
- 8.15 a.m.–4.30 p.m., in summer to 6.50 p.m.

The Royal Apartments of the House of Savoy occupy the right wing of the first floor—a sumptuous succession of carpets, tapestries, paintings and furniture.

Galleria d'Arte Moderna
- Tel. 055 238 86 16
- Daily (except 1st, 3rd and 5th Mondays and 2nd and 4th Sundays of the month)
- 8.15 a.m.– 1.50 p.m.

The gallery comprises 30 rooms providing an extensive overview of Tuscan painting from neoclassicism to the 1920s.

Galleria Palatina
- Tel. 055 238 8611
- Daily (except Monday)
- 8.15 a.m.–6.50 p.m

The Palatine Gallery displays the private collection of the Grand Dukes of Tuscany. You could spend days here among the Italian and foreign masterpieces of art from the 15th to 18th centuries.
They are hung in haphazard order: Titian, Van Dyck, Rubens, Raphaël, Fra Filippo Lippi, Bartolini, Velasquez, Murillo and more.

Museo degli Argenti
- Tel. 055 238 8709
- Daily 8.15 a.m.–4.30 p.m., in summer to 6.50 p.m.

The Silver Museum displays not only beautifully wrought silverware, but countless other treasures: gold, crystal, jewellery, ivory, semi-precious stones, furniture, porcelain and cameos, assembled by the Medici.

Museo delle Carrozze
- Tel. 055 212 557
- Closed for renovation (call just in case).

This small museum documents popular means of transport before the invention of the engine, with a collection of horse- and people-powered carriages and sedan chairs.

Galleria del Costume
- Piazza Pitti
- Tel. 055 238 8713
- Daily 8.15 a.m.–4.30 p.m., in summer to 6.50 p.m.
- Closed 1st, 3rd and 5th Mondays of the month, and 2nd and 4th Sundays.

Part of the collection of 12,500 costumes and 1000 accessories of the 17th to 20th centuries is displayed on a two-year rotation. Every six months, exhibitions are dedicated to one particular designer or a specific theme.

Giardino di Boboli C 6
- Main gate to the left of the Pitti Palace.
- Daily 8.15 a.m.–sunset; closed first and last Mondays of the month

This delightful park laid out over a hillside is full of birds, fountains and avenues of shady trees, with marble statues of angels, gods and mythical creatures half-hidden behind bushes—the atmosphere is magical. The first plans were drawn up around 1550 by a pupil of Michelangelo, Niccolò Pericoli, known as Tribolo. They were continued by Ammannati and then Buontalenti, and the garden was finally expanded in the mid-17th century by Alonso Parigi. At the top of the hill, above the amphitheatre,

The Boboli gardens, laid out on the hillside where the stones for the Pitti palace were quarried.

is the Casino del Cavaliere, housing the Porcelain Museum. Turning right after the amphitheatre, follow the avenue of cypresses to the Isolotto, an ornamental pond with the Fountain of the Oceans in the centre. Left of the amphitheatre is the Kaffeehaus, and further on a grotto designed by Buontalenti. Nearby, the Fountain of Bacchus depicts Cosimo I's favourite jester Morgante, astride a turtle.

Museo delle Porcellane

- Casino del Cavaliere
- Giardino di Boboli
- Tel. 055 238 8709

- Daily 8.15 a.m.–4.30 p.m.
- (to 7.30 p.m. in summer)
- Closed first and last Mondays of
- the month

In this small pavilion built for the son of Cosimo III, porcelain dinner services fit for royalty from the most famous factories (Meissen, Berlin, Vienna, Sèvres, Vincennes) are set out according to country of origin.

Forte del Belvedere

- Via del Forte di San Giorgio
- (off map by D 6)
- Daily 10 a.m.–4.30 p.m.,
- to 6.50 p.m. in summer.

Built to protect the Pitti Palace, this imposing bastion stands at the top of San Giorgio hill, affording a beautiful view of Florence, and the surrounding hills and valleys. The fort is now used for exhibitions of modern sculpture.

Giardini Bardini E 6
: Via dei Bardi, 1r
: Piazza dei Mozzi
: Tel. 055 290 112
: Daily 8.15 a.m.–dusk
The restored gardens of the Mozzi Palace: fruit trees, wisteria tunnel, 60 varieties of hyrangea, baroque flight of steps, mosaic fountains, English wood, azalea lawn and many other delights, as well as great views over Florence. There's an entrance from the Boboli Gardens, Costa San Giorgio 4; the ticket includes admission to both gardens, and the Porcelain and Silverware museums.

San Niccolò sopr'Arno F 6
: Via San Niccolò
This church, founded in the 11th century, was seriously damaged in the 1966 floods. A happy outcome was that the restoration revealed frescoes hitherto hidden by 16th-century altar paintings.

Torre San Niccolò G 6
: Piazza Giuseppe Poggi

The square, crenellated tower was built to defend the river in 1324. It was part of the third defensive wall around the medieval town, and has maintained its original height.

Piazzale Michelangelo
: (off map by G 6)
You can climb the steps from Piazza G. Poggi or take bus 12 or 13 up winding Viale Michelangelo to reach this wide terrace, to enjoy the view of Florence and the surrounding hills. In the centre stands the monument to Michelangelo, with a bronze reproduction of *David* and four of the Medici Chapel statues.

San Salvatore al Monte
: Via di San Salvatore al Monte
: (off map by G 6)
Michelangelo admired this church which he called "la bella villanella", the beautiful country-girl. Construction (1499–1504) was by Simone del Pollaiuolo, financed by the Guild of Calimala, whose business was the refining and dyeing of cloth and the importation of exotic goods. The sign of this guild, the eagle, is seen on the left side of the church.

San Miniato al Monte
: Via del Monte alle Croci
: (off map by G 6)

Daily 8 a.m.–12.30 p.m. and
2–7 p.m.; public holidays
8 a.m.–7 p.m.

St Minias, an early Christian martyred in the 3rd century under Decius, is said to have carried his severed head to the top of the highest hill south of Florence, and set it down on the site where this church was built in 1013. With its green and white marble façade, the church is a fine example of Florentine Romanesque, while the interior is richly decorated with inlaid marble, mosaics and painted ceiling. The marble-encrusted floor depicting the signs of the zodiac looks like delicate lacework.

The bell tower was built in the 16th century. During the siege of Florence, Michelangelo protected it from enemy fire by wrapping it up in mattresses and bales of wool.

Santa Maria del Carmine A 5

Piazza del Carmine

The bus from Piazzale Michelangelo meanders through delightful wooded scenery and past the Boboli Gardens. Stop off at Piazza Torquato Tasso to visit Santa Maria del Carmine. The church, begun in 1268, is modest in appearance but houses in the Brancacci Chapel some of the most important frescoes in Florence. They were commissioned from Masolino and his pupil Masaccio by a wealthy merchant in 1423. Masaccio died in Rome, aged 27, before his work was completed, and Filippino Lippi painted the final scenes. Masaccio's luminous colours, his expressive figures, his use of light and space all herald the Renaissance.

Santo Spirito B 5

Piazza Santo Spirito
Closed for restoration.

Brunelleschi designed this church for the Augustinian order, and it was continued by other architects after his death. The belfry is the work of Baccio d'Agnolo (1503). The shady little **Piazza Santo Spirito** (B 6) is very lively in the mornings (daily except Sunday, 7 a.m.–1 p.m.) when the housewives buy their fruit and vegetables at the market stalls. You will also find wooden articles made by local craftsmen and second-hand goods. In the evenings the area is best avoided.

San Felice B 6

Piazza San Felice

Dedicated to St Felix, the first bishop of Florence, the church has a fine Renaissance façade. The spacious interior exudes an atmosphere of peace and serenity. It houses a fine Crucifix of the Giotto school.

EXCURSIONS

If the city gets too hot, take off to the villas and gardens in the hills, or hire a car and explore the Tuscan countryside and its treasures.

Arcetri
- Pian dei Giullari
- (off map dir. D 6)
- Bus no. 38, or 30 minutes' walk from the Ponte Vecchio

The little hill-top town of Pian dei Giullari, which takes its name from the minstrels *(giullari)* who entertained the nobility of Florence in the 12th century, has many historic villas, including Il Gioiello, where Galileo spent his last years (via Pian dei Giullari 42).

The nearby **Arcetri Astrophysical Observatory** was built in 1872 and has the first solar tower built in Europe. At the top of the hill, **Villa Capponi** is known for its beautiful walled garden.

Villa di Castello
- Via di Castello, 47, Castello
- Road to Sesto Fiorentino
- (off map dir. B 1)
- Bus no. 2 or 28
- Tel. 055 454 791
- Daily 8.15 a.m.–sunset

This old fortress was remodelled into a villa by members of the Medici family in 1477. The garden, in the form of a series of terraces bordered by box and lemon trees, is open to the public. It was designed by Niccolò Tribolo at the beginning of the 16th century and has a famous fountain of Hercules sculpted by Ammannati.
Walk down to the bottom to see a grotto decorated with mosaics and shells, and a niche containing animal sculptures by Giambologna.

Villa della Petraia
- Via della Petraia 40, Castello
- Road to Sesto Fiorentino
- (off map dir. B 1)
- Bus no. 2 or 28
- Tel. 055 452 691
- Daily 8.15 a.m.–sunset

This 13th-century manor, nestling in the hills northwest of Florence, became a property of the Medici in 1530. It was renovated by Buontalenti who designed the symmetrical gardens, each geometrical shape neatly outlined by box hedges. The villa was the residence of Vittorio Emanuele II during the 19th century; some of the rooms are still richly furnished and you can admire an unusual collection of board games.
A lovely wooded park of oak, cedar, pine and plane trees stretches between La Petraia and the Villa di Castello.

Museo Stibbert

Via Stibbert 26
(off map dir E 1)
Bus no. 4 to Fabroni 3 stop
Tel. 055 486 049
Mon–Wed 10 a.m. – 2 p.m.;
Fri–Sun 10 a.m.–6 p.m.

Near the church of San Martino a Montughi, this museum in the home of collector Frederick Stibbert (1838–1906) displays the splendid objects he gathered on his travels in the Middle and Far East.

The rather eclectic collection includes the suit and cape worn by Napoleon I when he was crowned King of Italy, weapons and antique armour, rare books, games, maps, furniture, jewellery, fans and precious silks.

Fiesole

Bus no. 7
(off map dir. G 1)

Quite apart from its own charms, one of the principal attractions of this classical Tuscan hill town is the romantic view it commands over the green, often misty wooded slopes of the Arno valley to the city of Florence just 8 km (5 miles) to the southwest. Fiesole dates back to the 7th century BC, when it was one of the largest of Etruscan cities. It was later a Roman settlement and you can see the remains of the well-preserved theatre, dating from around 100 BC, and still used today during the summer festival.

In the town square, **San Romolo cathedral** with its crenellated bell tower was founded in 1028 and restored in the 19th century. The interior is Byzantine in inspiration. The **Bandini Museum** displays furniture, majolica ware, terracotta sculptures by Della Robbia, and paintings.

A steep lane takes you up to the church of **San Francesco** and its tiny monastery, built on the site of an ancient acropolis. The church has some interesting 15th-century works of art, and through the peaceful cloisters is a small museum devoted to Franciscan missionaries.

You can walk back down to town in a couple of hours. Stop on the way back to visit **San Domenico monastery**, where Fra Angelico took his vows. In the church is a beautiful altarpiece of the Virgin surrounded by saints, and the chapterhouse has a fresco of the *Crucifixion*, both by Fra Angelico. The road opposite the monastery, Via della Badia, leads you in a few minutes to the **Badia Fiesolana**, a cathedral which became an abbey in the 11th century and was transformed by the Medici during the Renaissance.

Villa and Park Demidoff
: Pratolino Via Bolognese
: (off map by H 1)
: Bus no. 25a

Buontalenti built a magnificent villa here for Francesco de' Medici, with a huge park full of statues and fountains. But it was left to abandon and the villa was demolished in the early 19th century. A rich industrialist, Prince Demidoff, had one wing restored as his own home in 1872 and the park laid out in English style. Giambologna's colossal statue of the Apennine, like a hoary rock surging out of the lake, is practically all that remains of the 16th-century park, along with the Pan fountain and Buontalenti's octagonal chapel.

San Salvi
: Via San Salvi 16
: (off map dir. H 3)

A few streets south of the Campo di Marte sports ground, San Salvi's refectory houses Andrea del Sarto's magnificent *Last Supper*, painted between 1519 and 1527. With its luminous colours and graceful depiction of the figures, the fresco is considered one of the most beautiful in the world.

Pisa
: 72 km (45 miles) west of
: Florence
: Hourly train from
: Santa Maria Novella
: station

Pisa's famous Leaning Tower and its other grandiose monuments of white marble are grouped

An engineering disaster, a triumph for tourism.

on the Piazza del Duomo, which also goes by the name of Campo dei Miracoli (Field of Miracles)—the 12th-century Duomo, the Baptistery and the tower *(campanile)*. Begun in 1173, the tower began listing in the sandy subsoil even before it was completed. Since 1992, the tilt—about 5 m (16 ft) from true upright—has been halted. Architects, engineers and geologists have collaborated to strengthen the foundations with a bolstering mixture of soil and cement and bind the base and lower tiers with steel cables. The tower has now been re-opened to the public. Also visit the cemetery *(camposanto),* the cathedral museum (Museo dell'Opera del Duomo), in the chapterhouse behind the Leaning Tower, and the San Matteo Museum, housed in a Benedictine monastery.

Siena

⋮ 48 km (30 miles) south of Florence
⋮ Intercity bus SITA

The steep and winding narrow streets of this town of red and pink brick all lead straight to its heart, the immense scallop-shaped Piazza del Campo, scene of the wild horse races of the Palio every July and August. The imposing Palazzo Pubblico contains 14th-century frescoes by Simone Martini and Ambrogio Lorenzetti. Also to be visited is the cathedral, famously striped with white and black marble, as well as its library and its museum, both richly endowed with medieval treasures. Housed in the Palazzo Buonsignori, the Pinacoteca assembles works by the great artists of the Sienese school.

San Gimignano

If you drive to Siena, make a detour (turnoff at Poggibonsi) to this marvellous medieval town bristling with tall, square towers. Walking through its narrow paved streets, it is easy to imagine yourself carried back in time. Visit the Collegiata, a 12th-century church decorated with frescoes by Ghirlandaio, the Palazzo del Popolo, whose frescoes show scenes of courtly love and of hunting, and the church of Sant'Agostino. Climb up to the Rocca, the citadel, from where the view across the countryside is sublime.

Lucca

⋮ 80 min by train from Florence
⋮ (on the line to Viareggio)
⋮ 20 min by train from Pisa

Kept safe and sound for centuries within its ramparts, the *centro storico* makes this gorgeous marble town one of the most attractive not only in Tuscany but in all of Italy.

The fortunes its merchants made out of silk and banking are visible today in superb churches, palazzi and villas, which were carefully preserved from destruction with a slush fund set aside to bribe foreign invaders to bypass the town. Today, the money still comes from textiles, but also shoes, paper-making, and agriculture producing, among other things, the highest quality olive oil. Start your tour with a walk along the top of the 16th-century fortifications. The complete promenade or Passeggiata delle Mura takes in 4 km (3 miles) around 11 tree-shaded bastions (baluardi) above grassy moats that offer a delightful setting for the town's summer music festival. To the southeast, Baluardo San Regolo is now a children's playground and gateway to the Botanical Garden with a 200-year-old Chinese ginkgo and an American sequoia.

The Romanesque cathedral, Duomo San Martino, seems to affirm the town's independent spirit by embedding its Lombard crenellated campanile in the Pisan-style porticoed façade, set beneath three tiers of polychrome marble arcades. Sculptures in the architrave of the north porch, Annunciation, Adoration of the Magi and Deposition, are attributed to Nicola Pisano.

Rising from the centre of the ancient Roman Forum, the exquisite Romanesque San Michele in Foro, begun in 1070, elevated its tiered arcades to give a loftier impact to the typical Pisan façade. There is a wonderful variety to the colour and design of its columns—scrolled, chevroned, striped and sculpted, in green, pink, white or black marble. Inside, see Andrea della Robbia's enamelled terracotta Madonna and Child on the first altar in the right aisle, and a Filippino Lippi painting of saints Jerome, Sebastian, Roch and Helen in the right transept. Half way along Via Fillungo, the shop-lined Piazza Anfiteatro (also called del Mercato) traces the elliptical shape of the ancient Roman amphitheatre. The houses have incorporated many of its 2nd-century brick arches. Southeast of the piazza is the street on which the wealthy Guinigi family built their homes from the early 1300s. One of the finest is the 14th-century tower-house of Michele, Francesco and Nicolao Guinigi, offering a splendid view from its battlemented top, now transformed into a miniature garden.

Housed in the 17th-century Palazzo Manzi, Via Galli Tassi 43, the National Museum includes paintings gathered from many Italian cities.

Dining Out

By nature, Florentines are conservative in many ways, and especially so when it comes to their food. Traditional dishes such as *crostini*, *ribollita* and *castagnaccio* have their roots in the Tuscan countryside. The same is true of the hearty vegetable soups, grilled meat, unsalted bread and Pecorino cheese. One of the great specialities is the well-known *bistecca alla fiorentina*, a huge steak grilled over charcoal, tender and full of flavour, cut from an animal less than two years old. The best come from Chianina cattle, raised in the Chiana Valley between Arezzo and Siena.

Below we have listed a number of restaurants where you will eat well at reasonable prices, together with some inexpensive trattoria, snack bars, cafés and famous *gelateria*. Note that many restaurants close in August.

CITY CENTRE

Antico Fattore D 5
Via Lambertesca 1/3
Tel. 055 288 975
Closed Sun
Trattoria just a few metres away from the Uffizi, serving traditional Tuscan dishes.

Birreria Centrale D 4
Piazza dei Cimatori 2
Tel. 055 211 915
Closed Sun
The "Central Brewery" specializes in dishes featuring goose, wild boar, pork and salmon, not to mention an amazing variety of vegetables and sauces—and beers.

Black Bar D 4
Via dei Calzaiuoli 107
Tel. 055 211 431
Closed Mon
Self-service and good for a snack, mainly pizza or tomato and mozzarella sandwiches.

Cantinetta Antinori C 3
Piazza Antinori 3
Tel. 055 292 234
Closed Sat and Sun
This elegant establishment is often packed, so get there early. Whether you choose a snack or a complete meal, you can be sure that all the produce comes from the Antinori farms. The wine, olive oil, bread and cheese are of excellent quality.

Donnini D 3–4
- Piazza della Repubblica 15
- Open daily

Extremely elegant café under the arcades, with a restaurant and American bar.

Festival del Gelato D–E 3
- Via del Corso 75

This is the *gelateria* with the largest choice in town—more than 80 flavours of ice cream and fun cornets in every colour under the sun.

Frescobaldi Wine Bar E 4
- Via dei Magazzini 2/4
- Tel. 055 284 724
- Closed Sun, and Mon lunch

A modern wine bar in an ancient street off the Piazza della Signoria: traditional dishes with the famous Frescobaldi wines.

Giacosa C 3–4
- Via della Spada 10
- Closed Sun

In the Roberto Cavalli boutique, among the rather chic stores in a prestigious street, this bar and tea room is the perfect place to recover from your shopping spree with drinks or coffee and cakes.

Gilli D 3–4
- Piazza della Repubblica 36–39
- Closed Tues

Typical Belle Epoque style café, with one of the most attractive and comfortable bars on the square. You can come just for a coffee, or have a leisurely apéritif, enjoy a cake or a light meal.

Giubbe Rosse D 3–4
- Piazza della Repubblica 13–14
- Open daily

Food for the body and the soul has been on offer here since 1890. Cultural events are organized in collaboration with the French Institute of Florence.

Il Cantastorie D–E 4
- Via della Condotta 7/9
- Tel. 055 239 6804

Humble but tasty food based on bread. Try the home-made pasta, a *ribollita* or *pappa al pomodoro* before tackling a tasty *fiorentina*.

Il Cavallino D 4
- Piazza della Signoria 28
- Tel. 055 215 818
- Closed Wed

An easy-going restaurant with a terrace overlooking Piazza della Signoria. No-one seems to mind if you sit reading for hours on end. The walls are decorated with photographs of old Florence. Quick and friendly service, and the food good—fabulous *penne* with lobster sauce.

La Borsa D 4–5
- Via Por Santa Maria 55
- Tel. 055 216 109

A snack-bar well known for its enormous vegetable or fruit salads, which make an ideal meal on hot summer days. Also sandwiches, pizzette and toasted sandwiches.

La Bussola D 4
- Via Porta Rossa 58
- Tel. 055 293 376
- Closed Mon in winter

An all-night pizzeria.

Le Botteghe di Donatello E 3
- Piazza del Duomo 28
- Tel. 055 216 678

Wholesome Tuscany cooking. Excellent *bistecca alla fiorentina* and good pizzas. Terrace overlooking the piazza.

Le Mossacce E 3
- Via del Proconsolo 55
- Tel. 055 294 361
- Closed Sat and Sun

Excellent for meat dishes like the famous *bistecca alla fiorentina*. Always very busy.

Marchetti D 4
- Via dei Calzaiuoli 102–104
- Tel. 055 210 805
- Closed Mon in winter

Self-service, known for its excellent pancakes and Russian salads.

Migone D 4
- Via dei Calzaiuoli 85–87

Pastry shop: sugared almonds of all shades, typical Tuscan cakes and local biscuits.

Oliviero D 4
- Via delle Terme 51
- Tel. 055 212 421
- Closed Sun

Open evenings only, this elegant restaurant is famed for its refined cuisine, reconciling regional traditions with innovative ideas. Freshly made pasta, delicious desserts and over 200 wines.

Ottorino D 3
- Via delle Oche 20
- Tel. 055 218 747
- Closed Sun

One of the oldest establishments in the city, now installed in newer and more airy premises. Rather formal, with crisp white tablecloths and attentive waiters in black suits. A good, varied menu.

Paoli D 4
- Via dei Tavolini 12
- Tel. 055 216 215
- Closed Tues

Two large vaulted halls covered in frescoes. Boisterous atmosphere, traditional food. The salads, mixed fresh in front of your table, are a work of art.

Paszkowski D 3–4
: Piazza della Repubblica 31–35
: Closed Mon
A bar and ice-cream parlour, this elegant establishment is especially renowned for its ices. Salads and pasta dishes are served but rather pricey.

Queen Victoria D 4–5
: Via Por Santa Maria 34
: Tel. 055 295 162
A very large self-service restaurant on two floors plus a garden in summer. It offers a choice of several pasta dishes, meat, fish and salads.

Rivoire D 4
: Piazza della Signoria 5
: Closed Mon
It isn't easy to find a free table in this bar in summer because of its delicious chocolate confections, not to mention the superb view of the piazza. Unctuous hazelnut cream served in glass pots, excellent fruit tarts and other Tuscan sweetmeats.

WEST

Baccus B 3
: Borgo Ognissanti 45
: Tel. 055 283 714
Classic cuisine, with an appetizing choice of meat or fish and ultra-fresh ingredients.

Baldini A 2
: Via il Prato 96
: Tel. 055 287 663
: Closed Sat, and Sun evening
An old traditional restaurant. Good cooking, generous portions.

Buca Mario C 3
: Piazza Ottaviani 16
: Tel. 055 214 179
: Closed Wed and Thurs lunch
In the cellars of Niccolini Palace, south of piazza Santa Maria Novella, this is a haven for anyone looking for traditional Florentine cuisine. The food is first-class.

Coco Lezzone C 4
: Via Parioncino 26
: Tel. 055 287 178
: Closed Sun, Tues evening and
: holidays
A small trattoria near the Palazzo Cortini. Authentic Tuscan dishes.

Creperia C 2
: Via dei Panzani 44
: Tel. 055 212 760
A wide choice of sweet and savoury pancakes, but also mouth-watering *crostini* (hot chicken livers on toast), sandwiches and pastries.

I Cinque Tavoli C 3
: Via del Sole 26
: Tel. 055 294 438
: Closed Mon

CAFÉS

Everywhere in Italy, but even more so in Florence, cafés are a local institution, a place where you can make a phone call, read the newspapers, buy stamps, ask directions —or just drink an excellent cup of coffee or a cappuccino and perhaps eat a quick snack. Usually there are a few tables, but the Italian habit is to stand at the bar and chat with the barman.

Only five tables in this small snack-bar, but there's nothing to stop you eating standing up. Excellent cheese *focaccia*, sandwiches and hamburgers. The beer is good and refreshing.

Il Gourmet A 2
: Via il Prato 68
: Tel. 055 294 766
: Closed Sun

A quiet restaurant, where portions are generous. Excellent pasta with wild boar, and noodles with a scrumptious mushroom sauce, best with the excellent house Chianti.

Il Latini C 3–4
: Via Palchetti 6
: Tel. 055 210 916
: Closed Mon

This place is always noisy and crowded, with communal tables and an open kitchen. Traditional country-style food.

La Carabaccia B 3
: Via Palazzuolo 190
: Tel. 055 214 782
: Closed all Sun, and Mon lunch

Tasty, innovative dishes, inspired by traditional Tuscan cuisine (*carabaccia* means onion soup).

La Spada C 3
: Via della Spada 62
: Tel. 055 218 757

Authentic Tuscan fare; popular with locals and very reasonable. Fabulous selection of spit-roasted and grilled meats.

NORTH

Cafe Caracol D 2
: Via de' Ginori 10
: Tel 211 427
: Closed Mon

For a taste of something hot and spicy, try this friendly Mexican restaurant and cafeteria.

Il Triangolo delle Bermude C 1
: Via Nazionale 61
: Closed Tues in winter

Unusual ice-cream specialities such as you have never tasted before: blue (a vanilla, aniseed and orange combination), rose flavour, and peanut.

Le Fonticine C 1
* Via Nazionale 79
* Tel. 055 282 106
* Closed Mon

A traditional atmosphere in this homely restaurant, with wooden ceilings and walls lined with paintings.

Robiglio E 2
* Via dei Servi 112
* Closed Sun

A renowned pâtisserie and tea room with a wide choice of fruit jellies, biscuits, confectionery and petits fours, both home-made and the best brands.

Sieni D 1–2
* Via dell'Ariento 29
* Closed Mon

A tea-room near the Central Market specializing in fruit tarts, liqueur tarts and in autumn, raisin bread.

Taverna del Bronzino
* Via delle Ruote 27
* (off map by E 1)
* Tel. 055 495 220
* Closed Sun

One of Florence's most popular restaurants, not far from San Marco. The menu is ambitious, offering interesting variations on traditional Tuscan recipes, and the portions are huge. Pricey.

Trattoria da Tito
* Via San Gallo 112
* (off map by E 1)
* Tel. 055 472 475
* Closed Sun

With photo-clad walls and well frequented by the rich and famous, this bistro is in the quieter part of town, not far from San Marco.

EAST

Acqua al 2 E 4
* Via della Vigna Vecchia 40
* Tel. 055 284 170
* Open every evening

Friendly atmosphere, and the whole meal is delicious from antipasti to dessert.

Calamai F–G 4
* Via dell'Agnolo 113
* Closed Wed

If you're feeling peckish round about teatime, head for this pastry shop renowned for its *cremini*, a brioche filled with custard cream; *cannoli*, cream-filled rolls; and Sicilian-style cassata (made from sweetened ricotta cheese and glacé fruits), as well as other magnificent cream cakes.

Dino G 4
* Via Ghibellina 51
* Tel. 055 241 452
* Closed Sun and Mon lunch

Dining Out

A comfortable restaurant where you can enjoy a Tuscan menu. Delicious *fagioli all'uccelletto,* a dish of beans and larks—yes, the feathered kind. The wine list comprises more than 300 different vintages.

Enoteca Pinchiorri G 4
- Via Ghibellina 87
- Tel. 055 242 777
- Closed all Sun, Mon lunch, Tues lunch

One of the most highly reputed restaurants of Florence, in a 15th-century palace. The owner is Italian, his wife French and together they cook up a highly original, memorable menu. The choice of French and Italian wines is incomparable.

Il Barrino
- Via V. Gioberti 71
- (off map by H 4)
- Tel. 055 660 565
- Closed Sun

A trattoria and wine shop that's very popular with locals. The steak and beef fillet are renowned.

Il Cibreo G 3
- A. del Verrochio 8
- Tel. 055 234 1100
- Closed Sun and Mon

An original restaurant near Piazza Ghiberti, inspired by nouvelle cuisine. On the other side of the kitchens, in the *vinaria*, the same menu is served at half the price.

Il Fagioli F 5
- Corso dei Tintori 47
- Tel. 055 244 285
- Closed Sat and Sun

An authentic Tuscan trattoria where you'll soon be made to feel at home.

Osteria del Caffè Italiano E–F 4
- Via Isole delle Stinche 11/13
- Tel. 055 289 368
- Evenings only; closed Mon

Opposite the Teatro Verdi, this is part wine bar, with snacks of cheese and dried sausage, and part restaurant offering high-quality Tuscan cuisine.

Osteria Semolina G 4
- Piazza Ghiberti 87
- Tel. 055 234 7584

Excellent value for money in this simple-looking restaurant: pasta, fish and meat dishes; incredible cakes and Neapolitan pizzas.

Vivoli F 4
- Via Isola delle Stinche 7
- Closed Mon

They claim that Florence's best ice cream is sold here. Fresh produce is used to make thousands of unusual flavours.

OLTRARNO

Cammillo C 5
- Borgo San Jacopo 57
- Tel. 055 212 427
- Closed Tues and Wed

A very lively atmosphere and a lengthy menu, in an interesting street a short walk from the Ponte Vecchio. The restaurant has many regular customers.

Cavolo Nero
- Via dell'Ardiglione 22
- Tel. 055 294 744
- Evenings only; closed Sun

In a narrow street, an intimate, romantic restaurant with starched white tablecloths. Refined cuisine, warm welcome.

Filipepe
- Via San Niccoló 39
- (off map by F 6)
- Tel. 055 200 13 97
- Evenings only

Modern and traditional cuisine with a strong Mediterranean accent, and pasta with vegetables.

Il Cantinone B 5
- Via Santo Spirito 6
- Tel. 055 218 898
- Closed Mon

An old, atmospheric cellar where you can enjoy traditional Tuscan cuisine.

TUSCAN WINES

Chianti is now a wine of worldwide reputation. If you are looking for a good DOCG chianti, then choose a bottle with the famous black cockerel or the *putto* (cherub) on the label. (Do not go looking for those fanciful raffia-wrapped bottles, or worse still, plastic imitations.)

Among other renowned Tuscan reds, Nobile di Montepulciano, Brunello di Montalcino, Brolio and Montecarlo are particularly noteworthy.

Among the whites, Vernaccia di San Gimignano is excellent, as is Bianco dell'Elba.

Il Santo Bevitore B 5
- Via Santo Spirito 64/66
- Tel. 055 211 264
- Closed Sun lunch

Lively trattoria that brings an original touch to traditional foods. Hand-made pasta, home-made cakes, plenty of vegetarian dishes, good choice of wines and reasonable prices.

La Capannina da Sante
- Piazza Ravenna,
- corner of Ponte di Verrazzano
- (off map by H 6)
- Tel. 055 688 345
- Closed Sun

Fresh fish prepared in unfussy ways, accompanied by a good selection of white wines. One of the best fish restaurants in Florence. Service on the terrace in summer.

La Loggia
- Piazzale Michelangelo 1 (off map by G 6)
- Tel. 055 234 2832
- Closed Mon

With a magnificent view of the rooftops, this is a special place, somewhere to go for a memorable first or last meal in Florence.

Mamma Gina C 5
- Borgo San Jacopo 37
- Tel. 055 239 6009
- Closed Sun

A friendly and welcoming trattoria offering typical Tuscan and Italian dishes. If you are lucky enough to be here in autumn, you can indulge in succulent dishes made from wild boar and hare, mushrooms and truffles—among Italy's best gastronomic treats.

Osteria del Cinghiale Bianco D 5
- Borgo San Jacopo 43
- Tel. 055 215 706
- Closed Wed

This is a small establishment with a friendly atmosphere, serving typical regional food.

Excellent meat dishes, wild boar and polenta.

Ringo's C 5
- Borgo San Jacopo 19
- Tel. 055 219 100
- Closed Sun

For a quick snack: excellent hamburgers, hot dogs and sandwiches freshly made to order.

Ristorante Ricchi B 5
- Piazza Santo Spirito 8/9
- Tel. 055 215 864
- Closed Sun

Fresh fish, with menu that changes daily. Reservation recommended. In elegant refurbished surroundings near Santo Spirito church.

Trattoria del Carmine A 5
- Piazza del Carmine 18
- Tel. 055 218 601

A long-established restaurant in a fairly quiet part of town. Inspired dishes made from fresh market produce. The terrace is particularly inviting on summer evenings.

Trattoria Vittoria
- Via della Fonderia 52 (off map by A 3)
- Tel. 055 225 657
- Closed Wed

Outside the centre, but it's worth the trip to sample this restaurant's fresh fish, simply prepared.

Entertainment

At night time, the streets of Florence are much livelier than in other Italian cities. Especially in summer, Florentines like to stroll around window-shopping or admiring the view, eat in a restaurant in the open air, or sit on a terrace watching the world go by.

THEATRE

The Tourist Office distributes a free magazine, *Firenze oggi*, which lists what's on at the theatres and the cinemas and provides all relevant information about festivals and other cultural events. *Firenze sera* and *Firenze Spettacolo* also publish detailed programmes for all events, shows, exhibitions and concerts.

Teatro Comunale
Corso Italia 16
(off map by A 2)
Tel. 800 112 211
Box office Tues–Sat
9 a.m.–1 p.m., and one hour before the show
Symphony concerts are held from February to April and from October to November; the opera and ballet season runs from December to February. From May to July, the May Music Festival.

Teatro della Pergola F 3
Via della Pergola 18
Tel. 055 22 64 1

Plays and the May Music Festival, concerts from January to April and from October to December in this very plush theatre.

Teatro Puccini
Via delle cascine 41
(off map by A 1)
Tel. 055 362 067
Concerts, alternative comedy, theatre companies and satire.

Teatro Verdi F 4
Via Ghibellina 99
Tel. 055 263 87 77
Musical comedies, revues, operettas, national ballets and recitals by well-known singers.

MUSIC

Andromeda D 4
Via dei Cimatori 13
Tel. 055 292 002
Closed Sun
A popular discotheque, frequented by the young Florentine crowd and tourists.

Full Up E 4
: Via della Vigna Vecchia 23–25
: Tel. 055 293 006
: Open from 11 p.m.
: Wed to Sat only
Sophisticated club, with piano bar. Not particularly suitable for the very young.

Jaragua
: Erta Canina 12
: (off map by F 6)
: Tel. 055 234 3600
South-American dancing for a refined, adult clientèle. In summer, terrace surrounded by greenery.

Jazz Club F 2
: Via Nuova de' Caccini 3
: Tel. 055 247 9700
: Open from 9.30 p.m.
: Closed Sun
A very friendly club.

Maramao G 4
: Via de' Macci 79
: Tel. 055 234 38 98
: Open 10.30 p.m.–2 a.m.
: Thurs to Sat only
Well-etablished disco-bar, different kinds of music every evening.

Space Electronic B 3
: Via Palazzuolo 37
: Tel. 055 293 457
: Open from 10.30 p.m.
: Closed Sun

Hi-tech disco with lasers, video and light-shows, karaoke and a pub.

Tenax
: Via Pratese 46, Firenze-Peretola
: Tel. 055 308 160
: Open from 10 p.m.
: Closed Mon to Wed
All the leading pop and rock groups appearing in Florence come here. Also other types of music.

Xo F 4
: Via G. Verdi 57
: Tel. 055 234 1529
: Closed Sun, Mon and Wed
All the rage. Discothèque, shows, concerts in a rave atmosphere.

Yab D 4
: Via de' Sassetti 5
: Tel. 055 215 160
: Open from 8 p.m.
: Closed Sun and Wed
Frequented by the fashion world, its most sensational disco evenings coincide with the fashion shows at the Palazzo Pitti.

CYBERCAFE

Internet Train D 1
: Via Guelfa 24
: Tel. 055 264 5146
Plenty of computers, scanners and printers for business, pleasure and keeping in touch.

The Hard Facts

Airports
Amerigo Vespucci Airport at Peretola, 5 km (3 miles) north-west of Florence, handles domestic flights and several daily flights to and from European cities. It is linked by bus to the city centre, terminus at Santa Maria Novella (10–15 min).

International flights also land at Galileo Galilei Airport at Pisa, 80 km (50 miles) west of Florence, just over an hour away by train.

Banks
In general, banks open Monday to Friday 8.20 a.m.–1.20 p.m. and 2.45–3.45 p.m.

All the big banks and post offices have automatic cash machines.

Climate
Located at the bottom of a basin surrounded by hills, Florence tends to get hot and stuffy in the summer, the warmest months being July and August with temperatures reaching 32°C (89°F) or more. Winters can be surprisingly chilly. The best times to visit are spring and autumn. Note, however, that at Easter the whole of Italy seems to home in on Florence (but you get the same impression in every Italian city).

Complaints
If you have a problem in a restaurant or shop, ask to talk to the manager.

The price of a porter or a drive in a horse-drawn carriage can always be negotiated in advance. If you think you are being overcharged for a taxi ride, consult the tariff which is displayed in the cab, but don't forget that various supplements are applicable at night, on Sundays and public holidays, and so on.

Consulates
UK: Lungarno Corsini 2
   Tel. 055 284 133

US: Lungarno A. Vespucci 38
   Tel. 055 239 82 76

Currency
The Euro (€), divided into 100 cents. Coins: 1, 2, 5, 10, 20 and 50 cents (centesimi), 1 and 2 €; banknotes: 5, 10, 20, 50, 100, 200 and 500 €.

Currency exchange offices, cambio, open Monday to Friday 8.20 a.m.–1.20 p.m. and 2.45–3.45 p.m., and some open on Saturday mornings. The office at Santa Maria Novella Station is also open on Sundays and public holidays (7.30 a.m.–8 p.m.). The exchange rate varies from one establishment to another. You can also change money in machines outside large banks and post office.

Electricity

220 V, 50 Hz AC is standard, with two-pin sockets.

Emergencies

Police (carabinieri): tel. 112
General emergency: tel. 113
Fire brigade: tel. 115
Medical emergency: tel. 118
Ambulance: 055 212 222
First aid: 055 436 1541
Stolen vehicles: 055 308 249
Tourist help line: 055 203 911

Duty chemists, 24-hour service (toll-free number 800 420 707):

All'Insegna del Moro
Piazza S. Giovanni 28r
tel. 055 211 343

Comunale n.13
Stazione Santa Maria Novella
tel. 055 216 761

Molteni
Via Calzaiuoli 7
tel. 055 289 490

Hospitals:

Azienda Ospedaliera Careggi,
Via Morgagni 85
tel. 055 427 7111

Mayer Children's Hospital
Via L. Giordano 13
tel. 055 56 621

Entry Regulations

You will need a valid passport to enter Italy, or, if you are a citizen of an EC country, a National Identity Card. Visas required for stays of more than 90 days.

Events

March: Fashion shows at the Palazzo Pitti; festival of the Annunciation in the Piazza della SS. Annunziata.

Easter Sunday: *Lo Scoppio del Carro* (Explosion of the Cart) Two white oxen draw a cart full of fireworks up to the cathedral.

April–May: Crafts exhibition at the Fortezza da Basso.

April–June: An exhibition of plants and flowers in the Piazza della Signoria and at the Uffizi.

Ascension: Grasshopper festival—caged grasshoppers on sale at the Cascine.

May: May Music Festival, with concerts, ballets and opera.

June: St John Festival with ball games in medieval costumes on Piazza Santa Croce. Fireworks in the evening on Piazzale Michelangelo.

June-August: Estate Fiesolana—music, theatre and cinema festivals.

September: Festa delle Rificolone—a procession with lanterns and candles by the Arno.

Autumn: Crafts exhibition at the Palazzo Strozzi.

October: Fashion shows at the Palazzo Pitti.

Christmas: Extensive display of *presepi* (figurines for Nativity scenes) and drawings in the Basilica San Lorenzo.

Finding your Way
Street numbers begin in the city centre, by the river, and increase as they go further out.

Horse-drawn Carriages
For a romantic ride, go to the cab rank in the Piazza del Duomo. But negotiate the price!

Lost Property
If you lose something in the street, go to the lost property office:

Ufficio Oggetti Smarriti
 Via Circondaria 17b
 Tel. 055 328 3942
 Open daily (except Sunday)
 9 a.m.–noon.

Objects left behind on the train are collected at the Santa Maria Novella Station:
 Tel. 055 235 21 90.

Post Office
The Italian postal service handles the mail and money transfers. It is not famed for speed, though the *Posta prioritaria* service seems to work quite well. Stamps are also sold in tobacconists and often in hotels. Mail boxes are red, sometimes with separate slots "for the city" and "all other destinations". For information call 160.

The post offices in Via Pellicceria and Via Pietrapiana are open Mon–Fri 8.15 a.m.–7 p.m. and until 12.30 p.m. on Saturday.

In Via Maso Finiguerra, the office is open daily 8.15 a.m.–7 p.m. All the other post offices open Monday to Friday 8.15 a.m.–1.30 p.m. and until noon on Saturday.

Public Holidays

1 January	Capodanno
6 January	Epifania/Befana
Moveable	Lunedì di Pasqua
25 April	Festa della Liberazione
1 May	Festa del Lavoro
2 June	Festa della Repubblica
15 August	Ferragosto
1 November	Ognissanti
8 December	Immacolata Concezione
25 December	Natale
26 December	Santo Stefano

Religious Services
Mass is celebrated in Italian. Florence also has a synagogue, as well as Baptist, Evangelist, Lutheran and Methodist churches.

Shops

In general, shops open from 8.30 or 9 a.m. to 1 p.m. and from 4 to 8 p.m. They close on Monday mornings except during the summer season, when they close on Saturday afternoons.

Taxis

You can hail a yellow taxi in the street, go to one of the taxi ranks or call a radio taxi company (Tel. 055 4390, 055 4499 or 055 4242). The fare (metred) is based on the distance, with extra charges for luggage, night journeys, etc.

Telephone

Public call boxes mostly require phone cards, which you can buy at the post office, in bars and tobacconists, at some newspaper kiosks, at the headquarters of Italian telecommunications (Via Cavour 21), and at the railway station. Note that the cards do not function until you tear off the corner. You can also make your calls from a public telephone centre, where you pay at the counter once the conversation is over. These centres are located at Via Cavour 21, in the post offices of Via Pellicceria and Via Pietrapiana, and at the railway station.

To make an international call dial 00, then the country code (US and Canada 1, UK 44), the area code without the initial zero, and the local number.

Directory inquiries: dial 12 40 or 892 424.

Tipping

Service charges are included in restaurants, but you can leave a few extra coins to show your appreciation. It is usual to tip the hotel porter, the doorman or anyone else who renders you a service.

Toilets

Public toilets (gabinetti) are often designated by the sign WC. If they don't have pictorial signs on the door, look for a U for men (uomini) and a D for ladies (donne).

Tourist Offices

APT (Agenzia per il Turismo)
Via Manzoni 16;
tel. 055 233 20
Mon–Fri 9 a.m.–1 p.m.

Province and City of Florence

Via Cavour 1r
Tel. 055 290 832
Mon–Sat, 8.30 a.m.–6.30 p.m.
Sun and public holidays
8.30 a.m.–1.30 p.m.

City of Florence

Borgo Santa Croce 29r
Tel. 055 23 40 444
Mon–Sat, 9 a.m.–7 p.m. (to
5 p.m. in winter. Sun and
public holidays 9 a.m.–2 p.m.

City of Florence
Piazza della Stazione 4
Tel. 055 212 245
Mon–Sat, 8.30 a.m.–7 p.m.
Sun and public holidays
8.30 a.m.–2 p.m.

Transport
The city centre is compact and easily walkable, but the bus is a handy way of getting to places such as Fiesole and the Medici villas. Ask for a free map at the ATAF office:

Ufficio Informazioni
Piazza Stazione Santa Maria Novella
Tel. 055 800 42 4500

The bus drivers do not sell tickets. You can buy them from automatic machines at the main bus stops, or at most newspaper kiosks, bars, tobacconists and the following offices:

ATAF, Piazza Stazione

CAP–COPIT, Largo F.lli Alinari 9

LAZZI, Piazza Stazione 4–5–6

SITA, Via Santa Caterina da Siena 15

A ticket valid for 70 min costs €1.20, valid 24 hours €5. A multiple ticket for four 70-min journeys costs €4.50. The PassePartour is a 24-hour bus pass that can be used on all the urban buslines and the red open-top double-decker CitySightseeing bus (route A through the city centre to Piazza Michelangelo; route B to Fiesole. It costs €22 for an adult, €11 for children up to 15. Write your name on the back. When you enter the bus, stamp your ticket in the red machine.

Four "ecological" minibus lines serve the city centre:

Line A, between Beccaria and Stazione Galleria via the cathedral, runs Monday to Saturday 8 a.m. to 8 p.m.

Line B runs along the north bank of the Arno between Piave and Vittorio Veneto, Monday to Saturday 8 a.m. to 8 p.m.

Line C serves the east part of the city, between Santa Maria Soprarno and San Marco, Monday to Saturday 8 a.m. to 8 p.m.

Line D serves the south bank of the Arno and crosses the Ponte Vespucci to the west part of the centre, between Ferrucci 1 and Stazione Galleria 1, daily from 7 a.m. to 9 p.m.

Water
Tap water is safe to drink. Fountains often carry a warning sign *Acqua non potabile* (not fit for drinking), but the one in the Pitti Palace courtyard is prized for its excellent water.

Index

GENERAL EDITOR
Barbara Ender-Jones
RESEARCH
Francesca Grazzi and Edris Rahimi
CORRECTION
Judith Farr
LAYOUT
Luc Malherbe
PHOTO CREDITS
Claude Huber: front cover, p. 11
A. Schroeder: inside front cover, pp. 1, 6, 31, 43, 51
Frances/hemis.fr: p. 2
Guiziou/hemis.fr: p. 5
Giraudou/hemis.fr: pp. 17, 22, 38
Corbis/Lees: p. 21
MAPS
Elsner & Schichor; JPM Publications

Copyright © 2007, 1997 by JPM Publications S.A. 12, avenue William-Fraisse, 1006 Lausanne, Switzerland
information@jpmguides.com
http://www.jpmguides.com/

Printed in Switzerland
Weber/Bienne – 10061.00.1052
Edition 2007

Say it in Italian

Greetings

The Italians appreciate your greeting them with a *"buon giorno"* (literally "good day") or *"buona sera"* ("good evening"). Save *"buona notte"* ("good night") for when you're off to bed. Add *"come sta?"* ("how are you?") and your Italian had better be good enough to understand the answer. With luck, your accent will give you away and

people will be kind enough just to answer *"bene, grazie"* ("well, thank you") and not give you a rundown on their ailments and tax problems. If they are the first to ask, reply: *"Bene, grazie"* and add: *"E lei?"* ("And you?"). The proper response to *"grazie"* by it-self is *"prego"* ("don't mention it"). Make your way through a crowded bus with a polite *"Per-messo"* ("May I?").

Men and women shake hands on a first meeting. With a woman, once you've struck up a friendship, exchange a light kiss on each cheek, usually an airy affair to avoid lipstick marks or misunderstandings. Down south, men commonly exchange a God-fatherly bear-hug. It's quite harmless.

DON'T BE SHY

To help you with your spoken Italian we provide a very simple transcription alongside the phrases. You may not end up sounding like a native speaker but people will be pleased to hear you trying. Syllables in capital letters should be stressed.

Good morning/ afternoon.	Buon giorno.	bwohn JOHR-noh
Good evening.	Buona sera.	BWOH-nah SEH-rah
Goodbye.	Arrivederci.	ahr-ree-veh-DEHR-chee
See you later.	A più tardi.	ah pyoo TAHR-dee
Hi!/Bye!	Ciao!	CHAA-oh
Yes/No.	Sì/No.	see/noh
Maybe.	Forse.	FOHR-seh
That's fine/Okay.	D'accordo.	dah-KOHR-doh
That's right!	Va bene.	vah BEH-neh
Please.	Per favore.	pehr fah-VAW-reh
Thank you/Thanks.	Grazie.	GRAA-tsyeh
Thank you very much.	Tante grazie.	TAHN-teh GRAA-tsyeh
You're welcome.	Prego.	PREH-goh
Nice to meet you.	Molto lieto.	MOHL-toh LYEH-toh
How are you?	Come sta?	KAW-meh stah
Well, thanks.	Bene, grazie.	BEH-neh, GRAA-tsyeh
And you?	E lei?	eh lay

Pardon me.	Mi scusi.	mee SKOO-zee
I'm sorry.	Mi dispiace.	mee dee-SPYAA-cheh
Don't mention it.	Non c'è di che.	nohn cheh dee keh
Excuse me…	Scusi…	SKOO-zee
My name is…	Mi chiamo…	mee KYAA-moh

I don't understand.	Non capisco.	nohn kah-PEE-skoh
Slowly, please.	Parli piano.	PAHR-lee PYAA-noh
Could you say that again?	Può ripetere, per favore?	pwoh ree-PEH-teh-reh, pehr fah-VAW-reh
Do you speak English?	Parla inglese?	PAHR-lah eeng-GLEH-zeh

I don't speak much Italian.	Non parlo bene l'italiano.	nohn PAHR-loh BEH-neh lee-tah-LYAA-noh
Please write it down.	Per favore, me lo scriva.	pehr fah-VAW-reh, meh loh SKREE-vah
I understand.	Capisco.	kah-PEE-skoh
Let's go.	Andiamo.	ahn-DYAA-moh

Getting around

Official metered yellow taxis line up at railway stations or outside the major hotels, only rarely hailed when they are on the move. Beware of pirate drivers, identifiable by the fact that *they* approach you. Unauthorized cars are called in Italian *abusivi,* which says it all. Expect legitimate extras on the meter price, charged particularly on night trips, on several pieces of luggage or on rides to or from the airport—rates are posted in the vehicle. Add a 10 per cent tip.

Public transport. Services for the bus *(autobus)* vary—they are good in Florence and Milan, overcrowded in Rome and Naples. The water-bus in Venice *(vaporetto* or smaller, faster *motoscafo)* is best of all—like a cheerful cruise along the canals through centuries of history. The number of the bus lines and the route served are displayed at each bus stop *(fermata)*. For cheaper fares, buy a book of tickets *(blocchetto di biglietti)* at news-stands or tobacconists. Get on through the door marked *"Salita"* and off at the exit marked *"Uscita"*. Subway trains, *Metro(politana)*, operate in Milan and Rome; the tickets are interchangeable with the bus system.

Trains. Besides the luxury international *EuroCity* (EC) and the *Intercity* (IC), there's the *Rapido,* faster than the crowded *Espresso*. The *Diretto* is slower and the *Locale* slower still, stopping at every halt, seemingly for anyone who cares to whistle it down.

English	Italian	Pronunciation
Taxi, please!	Taxi!	TAH-ksee
Are you free?	È libero?	eh LEE-beh-roh
Hotel Paradiso, please.	Hotel Paradiso, per favore.	oh-TEHL pah-rah-DEE-zoh, pehr fah-VAW-reh
To the airport/ the station, please.	All'aeroporto/ alla stazione, per favore.	ahl-lah-eh-roh-POHR-toh/ AHL-lah stah-TSYAW-neh, pehr fah-VAW-reh
I'm in a hurry.	Ho fretta.	oh FREHT-tah
Please stop here.	Si fermi qui.	see FEHR-mee kwee
Please wait for me.	Aspetti un momento, per favore.	ah-SPEHT-tee oon moh-MEHN-toh, pehr fah-VAW-reh
How much is it?	Quant'è?	kwahn-TEH
Keep the change.	Tenga il resto.	TEHNG-gah eel REH-stoh
Where is the bus stop?	Dov'è la fermata dell'autobus?	daw-VEH la fer-MAH-tah dehl-LA-oo-toh-boos
When does the next bus leave?	Quando parte il prossimo bus?	KWAHN-doh PAR-teh eel PROHS-see-moh boos
Where is the metro, please?	Dov'è il metrò, per favore?	daw-VEH eel meh-TROH, pehr fah-VAW-reh
A book of tickets, please.	Un blocchetto di biglietti, per favore.	oon blohk-KEHT-toh dee bee-LYEHT-tee, pehr fah-VAW-reh
one-way	andata	ahn-DAA-tah
round-trip	andata e ritorno	ahn-DAA-tah eh ree-TOHR-noh
first class	prima classe	PREE-mah KLAHS-seh
second class	seconda classe	seh-KOHN-dah KLAHS-seh
platform	binario	bee-NAA-ryoh
toilets	gabinetti	gah-bee-NEHT-tee
Is this seat free?	È libero questo posto?	eh LEE-beh-roh KWEH-stoh POH-stoh
strike	sciopero	SHOH-peh-roh

Accommodation

Your hotel lobby is where you first learn how much Italians like their titles. You'll get better service if you call the hall-porter or bell-captain *portiere*, as opposed to *facchino* (baggage porter or bellhop). Upstairs, the room maid is *cameriera*. Hotel tipping also has its fine distinctions: on the spot to porters for carrying bags or other incidental services, but a lump sum to room maids at the end of the stay.

Ratings for the hotel *(hotel* or *albergo)* range from luxury five-star to rudimentary one-star. Expect in-house laundry and dry-cleaning services only from three-star and better. Breakfast is generally optional (and not particularly copious) but in high season, resort hotels often insist on at least half-board. A separate rating system is used for boarding houses *(pensione)*, ranging from very comfortable, with excellent family cooking, to modest, providing just the basic services. Humble accommodation in monasteries run by monks is very different from the often luxurious amenities of converted monasteries run by hoteliers.

If you have checked out of your hotel, you can still take a *siesta* and bath in a low-price day hotel *(albergo diurno)*, usually close to the main railway station.

I've a reservation	Ho fatto una prenotazione	oh FAHT-toh oo-nah preh-noh-ta-TSYAW-neh
Here's the confirmation/voucher.	Ecco la conferma/il buono.	EHK-koh lah kohn-FEHR-mah/ eel BWAW-noh
a single room	una camera singola	OO-nah KAA-meh-rah SEENG-goh-lah
a double	una camera doppia	OO-nah KAA-meh-rah DOHP-pyah
twin beds	letti gemelli	LEHT-tee jeh-MEHL-lee
double bed	letto matrimoniale	LEHT-toh mah-tree-moh-NYAA-leh
with a bath/shower	con bagno/doccia	kohn BAH-nyoh/ DOHT-chah
Can I see the room?	Posso vedere la camera?	POHS-so veh-DEH-reh lah KAH-meh-rah
My key, please.	La mia chiave, per favore.	lah MEE-ah KYAA-veh, pehr fah-VAW-reh
Is there mail for me?	C'è posta per me?	cheh POH-stah pehr meh
I need:	Ho bisogno di:	oh bee-ZAW-nyoh dee
hangers	attaccapanni	attaka-PAN-ni
soap	una saponetta	OO-nah sah-poh-NEHT-tah
a blanket	una coperta	OO-nah koh-PEHR-tah
an (extra) pillow	un guanciale (in più)	oon gwahn-CHAA-leh (een pyoo)
This is for the laundry.	Questo è da lavare.	KWEH-stoh eh dah lah-VAA-reh
These are clothes to be cleaned/ pressed.	Questi sono vestiti da pulire/ stirare.	KWEH-stee SAW-noh veh-STEE-tee dah poo-LEE-reh/stee-RAA-reh
Urgently.	È urgente.	eh oor-JEHN-teh
I'm checking out.	Lascio l'albergo.	LAHSH-shoh lahl-BEHR-goh
I'd like to pay by credit card	Vorrei pagare con carta di credito.	vohr-RAY pah-GAA-reh kohn KAHR-tah dee KREH-dee-toh

Buon appetito!

The advantage of the ordinary *trattoria* restaurant over the more formal (and higher priced) establishment known as a *ristorante* is usually apparent as soon as you walk in. Much of the day's "menu" is appetizingly laid out on a long table or refrigerated counter. The display includes not only cold starters *(antipasti)* but also fish *(pesce)* or other seafood *(frutti di mare)* and even cuts of meat *(carne)*. State your cooking preference: *alla griglia* (grilled), *fritto* (fried) or *al forno* (baked). The *pasta* of course is in the kitchen, but these days it comes in hundreds of different shapes and sizes—manufacturers even have architects to design new forms to enhance the different sauces.

At midday, you may prefer the stand-up bar known as *tavola calda,* where you can get sandwiches and a hot or cold dish at the counter. Better than fast-food is the *panino ripieno,* a bread roll stuffed with cold meats, sausage, salad or cheese—your personal choice from the counter-display—the original of the American "submarine".

YOU AND YOU

There are several ways of saying "you" in Italian. *Tu* (plural *voi*) is familiar, used for children, friends, family. *Lei* (plural *loro*) is polite, for people you don't know well. And if you meet the person of your dreams, "I love you" is *Ti amo.*

English	Italian	Pronunciation
I'm hungry/thirsty.	Ho fame/sete.	oh FAA-meh/SEH-teh
A table for two, please.	Un tavolo per due, per favore.	oon TAA-voh-loh pehr DOO-eh, pehr fa-VAW-reh
The menu	Il menù	eel meh-NOO
The fixed menu	Il menú fisso	eel meh-NOO FEES-soh
I'm a vegetarian.	Sono vegetariano(a).	SAW-noh veh-jeh-tah-RYAA-noh(ah)
A glass of water.	Un bicchiere d'acqua.	oon-beek-KYEH-reh DAHK-kwah
I'd like a beer.	Vorrei una birra.	vohr-RAY oo-nah BEER-rah.
The wine list.	La carte dei vini.	lah KAHR-tah day VEE-nee
A bottle of red/white/rosé wine.	Una bottiglia di vino rosso/bianco/rosato.	oo-nah boht-TEE-lyah dee VEE-noh ROHS-soh/BYANG-koh/roh-ZAA-toh
beef	manzo	MAHN-dzoh
bread	pane	PAA-neh
butter	burro	BOOR-roh
cheese	formaggio	fohr-MAHD-joh
chicken	pollo	POHL-loh
coffee	caffè	kahf-FEH
fish	pesce	PEHSH-sheh
fruit juice	succo di frutta	SOOK-koh dee FROOT-tah
ice cream	gelato	jeh-LAA-toh
meat	carne	KAHR-neh
milk	latte	LAHT-teh
mineral water	acqua minerale	AHK-kwah mee-neh-RAA-leh
fizzy/flat	gasata/naturale	gah-ZAA-tah/nah-too-RAA-leh
mustard	senape	SEH-nah-peh
pork	maiale	mah-YAA-leh
salt and pepper	sale e pepe	SAA-leh eh PEH-peh
tea	tè	teh
vegetables	verdura	vehr-DOO-rah
The bill	Il conto	eel KOHN-toh

Telephone

You'll soon notice that on the telephone, the Italians do not reply with *Buon giorno* but *"Pronto!"* It means literally that the caller is "ready" to speak, a national characteristic. If you are answering the phone, in all likelihood, your next phrase should be *"Parla inglese?"* ("Do you speak English?") If the answer is *"No"*, try *"Qui parla..."* ("This is ... speaking").

Italy now has a modern, privatized telephone network, and just about everybody walks around talking into a mobile phone. Public telephones *(cabina telefonica)* function with phone cards, which can be purchased at post offices, some newspaper kiosks, the headquarters of Italian telecommunications and railway stations. They do not work until you tear off the corner. There are also Internet Cafés in every town, so you can keep in touch with your e-mails.

To call the US and Canada direct, dial 001. For the UK, the country code is 0044. Note that for local calls, you have to dial the whole number, including the initial 0.

May I use this phone?	**Posso usare questo telefono?**	POHS-soh oo-ZAA-reh KWEH-stoh teh-LEH-foh-noh
Can I reverse the charges?	**Posso telefonare a carico del destinatario?**	POHS-soh teh-leh-foh-NAA-reh ah KAA-ree-koh dehl deh-stee-nah-TOH-ryoh

---

HAPPY TALK

Enrich your vocabulary and sprinkle your conversation with a few useful, cheery adjectives: *simpatico* (charming), *splendido* (magnificent), *fantastico* (terrific), *formidabile* (tremendous), *divertente* (amusing), *piacevole* (pleasant), *allegro* (happy).

Wrong number.	Numero sbagliato.	NOO-meh-roh zbah-LYAA-toh
Speak more slowly.	Parli più piano.	PAHR-lee pyoo PYAA-noh
Could you take a message?	Può prendere un messaggio?	pwoh PREHN-deh-reh oon mehs-SAHD-joh
My number is…	Il mio numero è il…	eel MEE-oh NOO-meh-roh eh eel
My room number is…	Il mio numero di camera è il…	eel MEE-oh NOO-meh-roh dee KAA-meh-rah eh eel
Do you sell stamps?	Avete dei francobolli?	ah-VEH-teh day frahng-koh-BOHL-lee
How much is it to Great Britain/ the United States?	Quanto è per la Gran Bretagna/ gli Stati Uniti?	KWAHN-toh eh pehr lah grahn breh-TAH-nyah/ lyee STAA-tee oo-NEE-tee
I'd like to mail this parcel.	Vorrei spedire questo pacco.	vohr-RAY speh-DEE-reh KWEH-sto PAHK-koh
Can I send a fax?	Posso mandare un fax?	POHS-soh mahn-DAA-reh oon fahks
Can I make a photocopy here?	Posso fare una fotocopia qui?	POHS-soh FAA-reh OO-nah foh-toh-KAW-pyah kwee
Where's the mailbox?	Dov'è la cassetta delle lettere?	daw-VEH lah kahs-SEHT-tah DEHL-leh LEHT-teh-reh
registered letter	lettera raccomandata	LEHT-teh-rah rahk-kohm-mahn-DAA-tah
air mail	via aerea	VEE-ah ah-EH-reh-ah
postcard	cartolina postale	kahr-toh-LEE-nah poh-STAA-leh

NUMBERS

1 uno	6 sei	11 undici	16 sedici
2 due	7 sette	12 dodici	17 diciassette
3 tre	8 otto	13 tredici	18 diciotto
4 quattro	9 nove	14 quattordici	19 diciannove
5 cinque	10 dieci	15 quindici	20 venti

Money matters

Italy has adopted the Euro, and it makes life simple (it's just like using dollars). Coins are issued in denominations of 1, 2, 5, 10, 20 and 50 euro cents *(centesimi)*, 1 and 2 euros. Banknotes: 5, 10, 20, 50, 100, 200 and 500 euros.

The better exchange rate you get at the bank compared with the hotel is offset by the amount of time spent waiting in line, often one to make the initial transaction and another to collect the cash. Have your passport with you. In most places, banks are open Monday to Friday, 8.30 a.m. to 1.30 p.m. and another hour in mid-afternoon. Railway station and airport currency exchange offices stay open longer, and weekends as well. Most convenient of all – as long as you know your PIN – are the automatic cash dispensers for international credit cards (at stations and main tourist centres), but you will have to pay a commission.

QUESTION MARK	
To ask a question in Italian, all you have to do is change the inflexion of your voice, lifting it towards the end of the sentence:	
It's far away.	**È lontano.**
Is it far away?	**È lontano**?

bank	banca	BAHN-kah
currency exchange	cambio	KAHM-byoh
Where can I change money?	Dove posso cambiare del denaro?	DAW-veh POHS-soh kahm-BYAA-reh dehl deh-NAA-roh
Can you cash a travellers cheque?	Può incassare un travellers cheque?	pwoh een-kahs-SAA-reh oon "travellers check"
I want to change dollars/pounds.	Voglio cambiare dei dollari/ delle sterline.	VOH-lyoh kahm-BYAA-reh day DOHL-lah-ree/ DEHL-leh stehr-LEE-neh
Will this credit card do?	Accetta questa carta di credito?	aht-CHEHT-tah KWEH-stah KAHR-tah dee KREH-dee-toh
Can you help me?	Può aiutarmi?	pwoh ah-yoo-TAAR-mee
Just looking…	Sto solo guardando…	stoh SAW-loh gwahr-DAHN-doh
How much is this?	Quant'è?	kwahn-TEH
cheap	buon mercato	bwohn mehr-KAA-toh
expensive	caro	KAA-roh
Can I try it on?	Posso provarlo?	POHS-soh proh-VAHR-loh
I don't know the European sizes.	Non conosco le taglie europee.	nohn koh-NOH-skoh leh TAA-lyeh eh-oo-roh-PEH-eh
It's too big/small	È troppo grande/ piccolo.	eh trop-poh GRAN-deh/ PEE-koh-loh
I'll think about it.	Voglio pensarci.	VOH-lyoh pehn-SAHR-chee
I'll buy it.	Lo prendo.	loh PREHN-doh
A receipt, please.	Una ricevuta, per favore.	OO-nah ree-cheh-VOO-tah, pehr fah-VAW-reh
antique shop	antiquario	ahn-tee-KWAA-ryoh
bakery	panetteria	pah-neht-teh-REE-ah
bookshop	libreria	lib-reh-REE-ah
pharmacy	farmacia	fahr-mah-CHEE-ah
jewellery store	gioielleria	joh-yehl-leh-REE-ah
pastry shop	pasticceria	pah-steet-cheh-REE-ah
shoe shop	calzoleria	kal-tsoh-leh-REE-ah
supermarket	supermercato	soo-pehr-mehr-KAA-toh

Health and Safety

The best planned vacation may sometimes be spoiled—by a stomach upset or something of the sort. Too much sun, too much Chianti in the middle of the day and you'll be looking around for the chemists *(farmacia)*. One of them is open somewhere in town, even nights and weekends. Most often, it's located near the main railway station.

If you're prone to something that needs special medication, take a supply from home since, as good as most Italian medicine is, you may not be able to find precisely the same prescription on the spot. The emergency number to dial for first aid is **118**, and for an ambulance **113**.

Safety First. There's no need to be paranoid, but it's silly to take pointless risks. The precautions are simple, and the same as in big towns anywhere in the world. Leave your valuables in the hotel's safe *(cassaforte)* and carry only as much cash as you need. Keep your passport separate from your travellers cheques and credit cards. If you have rented a car, don't park it with bags visible on the seats. Always be on the alert for pickpockets in crowded places.

Police come in two kinds: *Vigili Urbani* (municipal police) in navy blue uniforms or all white in summer; and *Carabinieri* in brown or black, handling major crimes and street-demonstrations.

Emergency number for the police: **112**

I don't feel well.	Non mi sento bene.	nohn mee SEHN-toh BEH-neh
Where is a chemists?	Dov'è una farmacia?	daw-VEH OO-nah fahr-mah-CHEE-ah
an upset stomach	un'indigestione	oon-een-dee-jeh-STYAW-neh
an injury	una ferita	OO-nah feh-REE-tah
toothache	mal di denti	mahl dee DEHN-tee
headache	mal di testa	mahl dee TEH-stah
I feel pain…	Mi fa male…	mee fah MAA-leh
… in my leg	… la gamba	lah GAHM-bah
… in my arm	… il braccio	eel BRAH-choh
… in my stomach	… lo stomaco	loh STOM-mah-koh
… in my chest	… il petto	eel PEHT-toh
I am bleeding.	Perdo sangue.	PEHR-doh SANG-gweh
I need a doctor.	Ho bisogno di un dottore.	oh bee-ZAW-nyoh dee oon doht-TAW-reh
Can you give me a prescription?	Può darmi una ricetta?	pwoh DAHR-mee OO-nah ree-CHEHT-tah
Help!	Aiuto!	ah-YOO-toh
Stop thief!	Al ladro!	ahl LAA-droh
Leave me alone.	Mi lasci in pace.	mee LASH-shee een PAA-cheh
I've lost my wallet/ passport.	Ho perso il portafogli/ il passaporto.	oh PEHR-soh eel pohr-tah FAW-lyee/ eel pahs-sah-POHR-toh
My credit cards have been stolen.	Mi hanno rubato le carte di credito.	mee AHN-noh roo-BAA-toh leh KAHR-teh dee KREH-dee-toh
I'm lost.	Mi sono perso.	mee SAW-noh PEHR-soh
Where's the police station/the hospital?	Dov'è la polizia/ l'ospedale?	daw-VEH lah poh-lee TSEE-ah/ loh-speh-DAA-leh
I have been assaulted.	Sono stato aggredito.	SAW-noh STAA-to ahg-greh-DEE-toh
witness	testimone	tes-tee-MOH-neh
lawyer	avvocato	av-voh-KAH-toh

EVERY LETTER COUNTS

In Italian, every letter of the word is pronounced distinctly, so when a letter is doubled you have to pronounce it twice: *frutto* is "frut to", *delle* "del le", *birra* "bir ra", and so on.

NOTICES

The meaning of some signs you'll see:

Chiuso	Closed	*Signore (Donne)*	Ladies
Entrata (Ingresso)	Entrance	*Signori (Uomini)*	Gentlemen
Guasto	Out of order	*Uscita*	Exit
Occupato	Occupé	*Vietato*	Forbidden

FALSE FRIENDS

Many Italian words look like direct equivalents of English words, but you could be very wrong:

camera	room	*magazzino*	warehouse
conveniente	cheap, inexpensive	*moneta*	coins, change
fresco	cool	*morbido*	soft
incidente	accident	*pila*	battery (transistor)
libreria	bookstore	*slip*	underpants

JPM Publications • *Specialists in customized guides*

Neither the publisher nor his client can be held responsible in any way for omissions or errors.
Av. William-Fraisse 12, 1006 Lausanne, Suisse
Copyright© 2007, 1999 JPM Publications SA
www.jpmguides.com/ Printed in Switzerland – 10061.00.1052

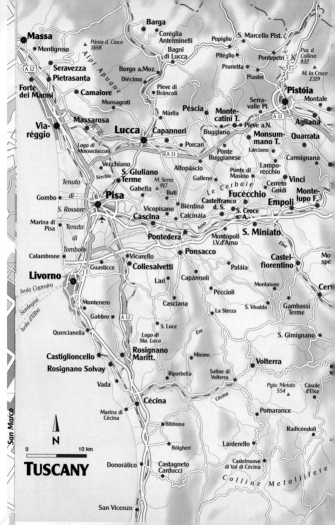

TUSCANY

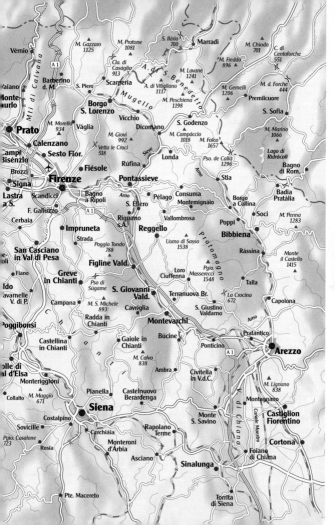